FOOD-BORNE ILLNESSES

Karen F. Balkin, *Book Editor*

Bonnie Szumski, *Publisher*
Scott Barbour, *Managing Editor*
Helen Cothran, *Senior Editor*

OPPOSING
VIEWPOINTS®
SERIES

GREENHAVEN
PRESS®

THOMSON

GALE

San Diego • Detroit • New York • San Francisco • Cleveland
New Haven, Conn. • Waterville, Maine • London • Munich

For more information, contact
Greenhaven Press
27500 Drake Rd.
Farmington Hills, MI 48331-3535
Or you can visit our Internet site at http://www.gale.com

LIBRARY OF CONGRESS CATALOGING-IN-PUBLICATION DATA

Food-borne illnesses / Karen F. Balkin, book editor.
    p. cm. — (At issue)
Includes bibliographical references and index.
ISBN 0-7377-1334-8 (lib. : alk. paper) — ISBN 0-7377-1335-6 (pbk. : alk. paper)
    1. Food-borne diseases. 2. Food poisoning. 3. Food—Microbiology. I. Balkin, Karen F., 1949– . II. At issue (San Diego, Calif.)
RC143.F657 2004
615.9'54—dc22
                                                                2003066265

Printed in the United States of America

Contents

Introduction

Laws in place today make meat processing the most highly regulated sector of the American food industry. Because contaminated meat has the potential to cause serious illness and even death among thousands of consumers, the development of an effective, federally regulated meat inspection program was a critical step in the prevention of food-borne illness in the United States. Indeed, America is now widely considered to have the safest meat supply in the world.

Beginning in the late 1800s, when exported salt pork and bacon were subject to inspection for trichinosis, federal laws have mandated the inspection of meat to prevent the spread of food-borne illnesses. Because meat is subject to contamination at many points during processing, careful inspection is necessary to ensure that consumers purchase a wholesome product free from food-borne pathogens. While the benefits to public health are undeniable, the passage of federal meat inspection laws has been surrounded by social, political, and scientific controversy for more than a century.

Heated debate followed the passage of the Meat Inspection Law of 1891. According to economist E.C. Pasour of North Carolina State University, this landmark legislation was not enacted to protect consumers from disease caused by contaminated meat. Rather, it was passed in response to unfounded charges by small meat packers that the large packers of the day—Swift, Armour, Morris, and Hammond—were selling unsafe beef. Pasour maintains that smaller slaughterhouses could not compete with larger houses and thus started rumors that the larger companies were selling tainted meat. The stories of unsafe beef frightened domestic buyers and ultimately harmed the export market. Soon, large and small meat packers alike were clamoring for federal meat inspection to prove to consumers that beef was safe to eat. The passage of the Meat Inspection Act of 1891, Pasour argues, was the federal government's political response to an economic problem, not a public health issue.

Less than twenty years after the Meat Inspection Act of 1891 was passed, an obscure Socialist writer published a novel depicting the supposed human degradation, animal cruelty, corruption, and filth associated with meatpacking. The novel stimulated cries for more government regulation of the industry. Upton Sinclair had hoped that his book, *The Jungle*, would focus attention on the evils of capitalism and the plight of oppressed workers. Instead, readers were appalled by the few pages he devoted to a description of the gory and unsanitary conditions under which meat was processed. "I aimed at the public's heart," Sinclair later wrote, "and by accident I hit it in the stomach." Demand for beef dropped as the book became increasingly popular. Beef exports were hurt as well. Winston Churchill, not yet prime minister of Great Britain, said that *The Jungle* "pierces the thickest skull and most leathery heart."

Most historians and Sinclair biographers agree that he spent little time in the Chicago slaughterhouses he called "Packingtown" and did not witness or even speak with people who experienced the horrors about which he had written. Whether *The Jungle* was an accurate description of slaughterhouses or not, it stimulated a public outcry that resulted in a congressional investigation of the meatpacking industry—and ultimately led to passage of the Meat Inspection Act of 1906. Then-president Theodore Roosevelt, who ordered the investigation, was skeptical of Sinclair and wrote in a letter to William Allen White in July 1906, "I have an utter contempt for him. He is hysterical, unbalanced, and untruthful. Three-fourths of the things he said were absolute falsehoods. For some of the remainder there was only a basis of truth." Despite his contempt for Sinclair and *The Jungle*, Roosevelt signed the Meat Inspection Act along with the Pure Food and Drug Act (which banned adulterated food and unsafe patent medicine) on June 30, 1906.

Lawrence W. Reed of the Mackinac Center for Public Policy argues that the Meat Inspection Act of 1906, like the act passed in 1891, had less to do with public health and more to do with profits. He writes: "When the sensational accusations of *The Jungle* became worldwide news, foreign purchases of American meat were cut in half and the meatpackers looked to new regulations to give their markets a calming sense of security." Nevertheless, despite the fact that the new legislation was passed mainly out of economic considerations and cost the taxpayers of the day $3 million, it did provide for more meat inspectors, new regulations for smaller slaughtering operations, and stricter regulations for larger facilities. Consumers were satisfied that Roosevelt had responded to the will of the people and used the power of the federal government to ensure a safer meat supply.

The Poultry Products Inspection Act of 1957 (which added the inspection of interstate-bound poultry to the list of federal inspection responsibilities) and the Wholesome Meat Act of 1967 and the Wholesome Poultry Act of 1968 (both involved scrutiny of plant facilities and processes, not just carcasses) marked the only changes in meat inspection laws for the next ninety years. Trained inspectors continued to rely on their experience and the "poke and sniff" method to determine the wholesomeness of meat. If meat moving down a slaughterhouse packing line looked fresh and wholesome, did not smell as if it were spoiled, or feel spongy or slimy, it was given a U.S. Department of Agriculture (USDA) approval stamp. Unfortunately, the "poke and sniff" method could not detect the presence of *Salmonella* or *E. coli*, two food-borne pathogens that can sicken and even kill consumers.

The inherent limitations of the "poke and sniff" inspection method eventually had fatal consequences. A deadly outbreak of *E. coli* in 1993 was traced to undercooked hamburgers eaten at a Jack in the Box restaurant in the Pacific Northwest. Hundreds of people in the area became ill and several children died. USDA guidelines and consumer education materials were revised, now recommending that processed beef be cooked at a higher temperature to kill *E. coli*. However, consumer organizations like Safe Tables Our Priority (STOP), an activist group started by the mothers of children who had died in the Jack in the Box *E. coli* outbreak, demanded more. According to STOP, "After numerous, substantive contacts with USDA officials . . . S.T.O.P. became a key player in facilitating the first meat and poultry inspection reforms in over 90 years; reforms that included microbial testing for animal fecal contamination [the source of *E. coli*]."

The federal government again responded to a public outcry for safer meat, and in 1996, then-president Bill Clinton made the Hazard Analysis and Critical Control Points (HACCP) system part of a new inspection law. The HACCP system involves identifying points in a processing plant where contamination is most likely to occur and finding methods to prevent it. Each plant can design its own HACCP system but must meet certain federal standards. Then-secretary of agriculture Dan Glickman said, "Rather than catching problems after they occur, we will now focus on preventing problems in the first place." A key point in the HACCP system involves microbiological tests of raw meat and poultry to detect *E. coli* and *Salmonella*. Clinton said at the time, "These new meat and poultry contamination safeguards will be the strongest ever. They are flexible and they do challenge the private sector to take responsibility. They also use the most up-to-date science to track down invisible threats."

Although the HACCP system represented a vast improvement over the Meat Inspection Act of 1906, critics insisted that it did not go far enough. Under the HACCP, company workers were expected to keep records of how well the system was working. For example, companies were required to test for *E. coli*, but no federal inspector would oversee the tests or the final results. In a June 30, 2000, decision (*American Federation of Government Employees et al., v. the U.S. Department of Agriculture et al.*), the U.S. Court of Appeals for the District of Columbia Circuit ruled that it was the duty of federal employees—USDA employees not meatpacking plant employees— to determine whether a product was adulterated or unadulterated. The Court of Appeals ruled unanimously that federal inspectors have a statutory duty to examine meat and poultry carcass-by-carcass.

The passage of federal meat inspection laws over the past century represents the government's most significant effort at preventing food-borne illnesses. In *At Issue: Food-Borne Illnesses*, authors consider the causes of and evaluate possible solutions to this ongoing public health threat.

1

Food-Borne Illnesses: An Overview

Rick Linsk and Gita Sitaramiah

Rick Linsk and Gita Sitaramiah are reporters for the Pioneer Press *in Minnesota.*

Nationally, two out of every five cases of food-borne illness begins with restaurants or caterers. The poor hand-washing practices of restaurant employees spread many types of illness, such as hepatitis A. The presence of other disease-causing organisms such as *E. coli, Salmonella,* and *Listeria,* is usually the result of fecal contamination of meat during processing. Poor food-handling procedures, such as not cooking meat at a temperature high enough to kill pathogens or failing to keep food cold enough to prevent bacteria growth, also cause food-borne illnesses.

Tracie Eckstrom's friends still rib her: She should have had a beer. Relaxing at the Hoggsbreath Bar & Restaurant in Little Canada, [Minnesota] after a softball game in March [2000], Eckstrom was the only team member who drank a glass of ice water. And she was the only one in her group who got hepatitis A.

Thanks to an infected cook who used the bathroom and failed to adequately wash his hands, Eckstrom and 38 other people contracted the virus, which causes nausea, fever, stomach cramps and malaise. An estimated 2,000 people were exposed at the popular sports bar, and more than 800 lined up for protective shots.

Outbreaks of food-borne illness are becoming increasingly familiar.

About 25 times a year on average, public health agencies in Minnesota hear about groups of people getting sick after eating at restaurants, catered events, church picnics, schools, private parties and other venues. The rate is about the same in Wisconsin.

Government-investigated outbreaks barely scratch the surface of food-borne illness in the United States. Most of the estimated 76 million people who get sick annually from something they ate, including 500,000 in Minnesota, never become known to public health agencies.

Still, a look at the records of known outbreaks provides insights into where and how Americans are getting sick, and what can be done about it.

Trends suggest cause for concern, even as public health agencies wield sophisticated new tools to trace and stamp out food-borne disease. For example:

Minnesota's reported outbreaks have increased sharply in recent years. Better detection techniques are one reason, but experts also point to new or evolving germs taking advantage of changes in our diets, the way food is produced, and a more vulnerable population. Some health researchers fear the United States is on the verge of a food-borne illness epidemic.

Restaurants and catered events—not backyard picnics or grocery stores—are the most common places where reported outbreaks start. Many are caused by restaurant employees who come to work sick or handle food improperly.

Most food-borne illness victims suffer for only a few days, but some cases end in tragedy. In July [2000], a 3-year-old South Milwaukee, [Wisconsin] girl died from kidney failure in an *E. coli* outbreak that investigators linked to contaminated ground beef. Last year [1999], a Rochester [Minnesota]–area man died in an outbreak involving deli meats contaminated with *Listeria*.

Most outbreaks remain hidden from the public, meaning you may walk into a restaurant and not know others have been ill. State and local officials say they announce outbreaks only when there's a risk that illnesses still are spreading.

Health investigators from Minnesota, Wisconsin and the federal government have traced outbreaks to a variety of weak links in the food chain, from contaminated ingredients to malfunctioning equipment to mistakes by kitchen workers. Outbreaks can strike at well-run restaurants whose employees make one crucial mistake, or at dirty establishments rife with unsafe practices. Home cooks can unwittingly start outbreaks in their own kitchens or at community events, too.

In Minnesota and Wisconsin, half the outbreaks in recent years began with restaurants or caterers. They were the leading source nationally as well, starting two of every five reported outbreaks from 1988 to 1997, according to the U.S. Centers for Disease Control and Prevention. Cooks at home were to blame one of every five times, the CDC said. Experts believe the numbers may be skewed because food-borne illness victims are more likely to complain about a restaurant than about themselves, their church or a private club.

Loyalty tested

"DRINKIN DANCIN EATIN," announces the sign outside the Hoggsbreath. Another near the front door warns against parking motorcycles on the sidewalk. The Rice Street sports bar might not be associated with gourmet food, but its devoted clientele reminds people of the television show "Cheers": a place where everyone knows your name.

Just a few months ago on a typical day, 400 to 500 people came for breakfast, lunch, dinner, live music or to hang out after sports, as Tracie Eckstrom did. That, however, was before the outbreak that nearly put an end to owners Tom and Jocelyn Duray's business of 24 years.

The trouble began on March 10 [2000], when a manager at Hoggsbreath sent home a cook who was not feeling well. But the cook returned to work a few days later after an emergency room doctor misdiagnosed the problem as a respiratory condition.

It was a mistake that would eventually have serious consequences for Eckstrom, the Durays and hundreds of other Hoggsbreath customers.

The next week, the cook—still not feeling well—developed jaundice, a noticeable yellowing of the skin. This time, a doctor ordered lab tests. On March 20, four days after Eckstrom ate her fateful dinner of a submarine sandwich and a glass of water, the results confirmed that the cook was infected with hepatitis A.

Some health researchers fear the United States is on the verge of a food-borne illness epidemic.

Hepatitis A can make someone sick up to seven weeks after exposure, and hundreds of people had been exposed.

Health officials announced the outbreak to the public on April 14, and more than 800 people lined up in the next few days for protective immune globulin shots at a special public health clinic.

For Tracie Eckstrom, the shots, which are only effective if given within two weeks of exposure, came too late. During Easter weekend in late April, she came down with the classic symptoms of hepatitis A: a 102-degree fever, malaise, nausea, and cramps, followed by jaundice. A lab test confirmed she had the virus, leaving her in tears.

A computer-support technician who has no sick-pay benefits, Eckstrom was out of work for two weeks and says she remained fatigued for six weeks. She joined a class-action lawsuit against Hoggsbreath.

"I never want to see a business go out of business. . . . But maybe they should've been a little more aware of what they were doing," she said.

Hoggsbreath co-owner Tom Duray makes no excuses for the outbreak. "As a business owner, you're responsible for your employees and what happens in your establishment," he said.

By all accounts, the Durays have worked hard to repair the damage to customers' loyalty. After the outbreak, the establishment's future was questionable, but business is now back to about 60 percent of normal. The restaurant's insurance company covered many customers' medical expenses. Workers now wash their hands whenever they enter the kitchen and wear latex gloves as a second line of defense, Tom Duray said. Health officials add that the owners were extremely cooperative with them throughout the outbreak and investigation. Jocelyn Duray herself was ill with the virus for about 10 days.

The cook, meanwhile, left the Hoggsbreath for another restaurant job. Citing privacy laws, health officials refused to identify him.

Unclean hands

It's unlikely anyone will ever know exactly how Eckstrom or others got the virus at Hoggsbreath.

But because of the way that the virus is transmitted—excreted in the feces of infected people—officials are certain that the cook must have accidentally contaminated food.

When a cook or server fails to properly wash hands after using the bathroom, even a microscopic amount of fecal matter can spread bacteria or viruses to food, plates, silverware, co-workers or customers. It happens more than you might realize.

"Our society in general (does) a very poor job" of washing hands, said Kirk Smith, state Health Department epidemiologist. "I notice it in public restrooms. A three-second hand-washing is not going to do the job."

Ill or infected food workers figured in one of every three outbreaks in Minnesota from 1989 to 1998, according to a *Pioneer Press* analysis of 200 confirmed outbreaks. Likewise, a Minnesota Health Department study found that infected food workers were associated with more than half the outbreaks of viral gastroenteritis—the so-called stomach flu—in the past two decades. Sometimes the food handlers themselves had been sick; in other cases, they had household members who were ill. Viral infections are the leading cause of outbreaks in Minnesota.

Three different Subway shops in Minnesota had viral outbreaks that investigators tied to infected employees—in Redwood Falls in January 1996, a month later in Bloomington, and in 1998 in Minneapolis. In the Bloomington case, 21 members of a men's chorus reported getting sick about a day after sharing three six-foot sandwiches. An employee who made the sandwiches had a child ill with diarrhea the week before.

In 1998, investigators concluded an infected food handler had contaminated the seafood bowtie salad, starting an outbreak of *shigella* bacteria among 30 people at Ciatti's Restaurant in Edina [Minnesota]. In July, a Hennepin County jury ordered the restaurant's former ownership—it has changed since the outbreak—to pay $140,000 to lawyer Cecil Schmidt and his wife Barbara. Schmidt's son Jeffrey was hospitalized and settled a separate lawsuit.

Sick workers should not even be in a restaurant. Minnesota law requires restaurants to excuse employees who are ill with vomiting or diarrhea, or infected with *salmonella, shigella, E. coli* or hepatitis A. But there are powerful incentives for restaurant workers—often low-paid and lacking benefits like sick pay—to come to work ill. Some sick employees, like the cook at Hoggsbreath, are infectious before their symptoms appear.

Painful mistakes

After sick workers, unsafe food handling is the next most common cause of outbreaks. In one of every four cases, outbreaks stemmed from undercooking meat, not maintaining food at proper temperatures, cross-contaminating foods with bacteria from raw meat or poultry, or other poor practices.

Health officials investigating a *salmonella* outbreak at the Perkins Family Restaurant in Eagan, [Minnesota] in 1997 found eggs stored above recommended safe temperatures. Investigators detected *salmonella* on a cutting board, near a cooking area, in a pork chop, and in the stool samples of three employees. They theorized the illnesses came from ill employees or contaminated food-preparation surfaces. *Salmonella*, commonly found on raw or undercooked meats, poultry and in eggs, is the bacteria most often associated with outbreaks nationwide.

At a Perkins in Alexandria, [Minnesota] inspectors discovered numerous problems after 25 employees and 25 patrons tested positive for the *salmonella heidelberg* bacteria in July 1999. Employees did not routinely wash their hands between handling frozen raw chicken and making salads, and the hand washing sink was not near the cook line, according to a state report. The restaurant made several changes, replacing worn cutting boards and using pasteurized eggs for omelets.

Vivian Brooks, a spokeswoman for Perkins, said the chain operates every day, around the clock, at 500 restaurants in 35 states, with high standards and happy customers.

In about one of every 10 [food-borne illness] outbreaks studied, illnesses stemmed from contaminated foods.

"These situations that you're describing are not typical," she said.

Lantern House, a Chinese restaurant in Duluth, [Minnesota] had the misfortune in 1998 of making some important people sick: four employees of the St. Louis County Public Health Department, who became ill about six hours after eating at the buffet-style restaurant.

Investigators noted "extensive" violations of food-safety standards and blamed the illnesses on *bacillus cereus*, a pathogen that grows when foods, especially rice, are not kept hot enough. In fact, as the health officials reported after two inspections, "No food item was properly cooled or heated." Authorities closed the restaurant as a health emergency, and it never reopened.

Private events started 33 outbreaks in the period studied, including three at community potluck dinners.

Health officials believe food-handling practices are riskier at the potlucks than at restaurants. But earlier this year [2000], state legislators passed a new law to exempt publicly advertised potluck dinners from licensing and inspection rules. Proponents said they were defending a Minnesota tradition from overzealous bureaucrats.

Publicity rare

Outbreaks can destroy restaurants, which is one reason government agencies do not routinely tell the public about them. Aggie Leitheiser, an assistant commissioner for the Minnesota Health Department, said outbreaks are publicized when officials believe illnesses still may be spreading, as in the Hoggsbreath case.

Craig Hedberg, a former epidemiologist for the state Health Department and now a professor at the University of Minnesota's School of Public Health, said restaurant operators and employees are more likely to cooperate with investigators if they don't fear being stung by bad publicity.

Tom Day, government affairs director for Hospitality Minnesota, a restaurant trade group, said publicizing outbreaks as they occur doesn't do anyone any good. The industry would not oppose an annual report listing where outbreaks had occurred.

"I think they could be publicized on an informational basis after all the facts and findings are known," Day said. "I don't think it's fair to hang a restaurant before everything is known."

Tainted on delivery

In about one of every 10 outbreaks studied, illnesses stemmed from contaminated foods.

In some of those cases, careful measures might have prevented illnesses. When a kitchen worker made salads without washing the lettuce last August [1999] at Clyde's on the St. Croix, a Bayport [Minnesota] restaurant, an estimated 100 to 150 diners became ill with a food-borne virus. The worker did not wash the lettuce because a label on the produce box "purportedly stated this item was a pre-washed lettuce," said a report by Washington County health investigators.

Earlier this year [2000], an *E. coli* outbreak among students at a Minneapolis middle school was traced to a casserole of ground beef, pasta and tomato sauce. State health officials said the meat probably was undercooked. As much as 80 percent of the raw hamburger in the United States is contaminated with *E. coli* bacteria, but cooking to 160 degrees can kill it.

In a few instances, outbreaks occurred despite precautions. Hundreds of Minnesotans in 1998 were caught up in an international series of outbreaks from parsley. The parsley, contaminated with *shigella* at a farm in Mexico, survived washing by restaurants. Some restaurants also innocently made matters worse by chopping the parsley, spreading the bacteria further.

In at least two of the eight seafood-related outbreaks documented in Minnesota since 1989, diners were made ill by hard-to-detect toxins. Four diners got *ciguatera* poisoning in 1997 from hogfish at Bluepoint Restaurant in Wayzata. The same year, five people were sick from *scombroid* poisoning, also known as histamine poisoning, from Indonesian tuna served at Billabong's Restaurant in Bloomington.

Perhaps the most alarming, though rare, are the outbreaks associated with processed, nationally distributed products.

In 1998, *Listeria*-tainted hot dogs and lunch meats from a Sara Lee plant in Michigan killed 21 people in the United States and sickened 80 more.

Last year [1999], a 55-year-old chemistry professor died and four other people became ill after ingesting *Listeria* in cold-cut deli meats purchased from a HyVee grocery store in Rochester, [Minnesota].

What frightens and challenges public health officials is the way that food-safety mistakes these days can become crises of immense proportions.

Six years ago, 224,000 people nationwide were infected with *salmonella* after eating Schwan's ice cream, shipped from Minnesota in tanker trailers that had previously carried nonpasteurized eggs.

Dr. Michael T. Osterholm, the former Minnesota state epidemiologist and an internationally recognized expert in infectious diseases, called the outbreak "a harbinger of things to come."

2

Mad Cow Disease Is a Threat to American Meat

Peter Lurie

Peter Lurie is a physician, public health researcher, and the deputy director of Public Citizen's Health Research Group.

The United States has not been aggressive enough in the fight against mad cow disease. Unless the government becomes more vigilant, the disease will likely find its way into America's food supply. Immediate action by the Food and Drug Administration (FDA) is required to regulate dietary supplements, which may contain infected bovine materials imported from countries where mad cow disease has been diagnosed. The FDA must also insist on stricter compliance with the ban against commingling feed intended for ruminants (cattle, goats, and sheep) with feed intended for nonruminants. Feeding ruminant parts to ruminants was how the mad cow disease epidemic spread in England. Finally, the U.S. Department of Agriculture should test the brain tissue of more cows exhibiting neurological symptoms at the time of slaughter.

While the U.S., to the best of our knowledge, remains free of both Bovine Spongiform Encephalopathy (BSE), otherwise known as "Mad Cow Disease," as well as its human counterpart, variant Creutzfeldt-Jacob Disease (vCJD), the experiences of European countries that grew complacent and now are suffering from epidemics of BSE and, in some cases, vCJD should make us more vigilant than we are at present. The agent that causes BSE has often found a way to pierce small chinks in the public health armor. For this reason, it is critical not only to maintain our defenses but also to strengthen them in the several areas I will highlight in this testimony.

I will address four areas:
1. How the agent that causes BSE might enter the country;
2. How the agent, if it entered the country or arose spontaneously within the country, could spread;
3. Whether the U.S. is doing enough testing to detect the disease; and

Peter Lurie, testimony before the Senate Commerce, Science, and Transportation Committee, Subcommittee on Consumer Affairs, Foreign Commerce, and Tourism, Washington, DC, April 4, 2001.

4. Whether there are medical practices that might spread the disease. How could the BSE agent enter the country?

How the agent that causes BSE might enter the country

We have serious concerns about the ability of customs inspectors to adequately police the borders. With the dramatic increase in global trade, the workload of these inspectors is only likely to grow. Transhipments between countries can make determining the origin of meat and bone meal quite difficult. This is, of course, an issue that extends well beyond BSE to encompass broader issues of food safety.

An issue of particular concern is that of dietary supplements. In 1994, the government, unwisely, essentially deregulated the dietary supplement industry. Whereas, prior to the Dietary Supplement, Health and Education Act (DSHEA), the industry had the burden of demonstrating the safety of its products, now the Food and Drug Administration (FDA) must demonstrate that a particular dietary supplement is unsafe before it can take action. Moreover, this now-$14 billion industry is not required to prove the efficacy of its products and the FDA has still failed to issue Good Manufacturing Practice (GMP) regulations for dietary supplements four years after the agency commenced rulemaking on this issue and seven years after DSHEA. Manufacturers are not required to register with the FDA and the agency only inspects approximately 1% of imported items subject to its jurisdiction, a fraction that may be still lower for dietary supplements. The agency has issued an Import Alert for materials sourced from BSE countries, but compliance is voluntary.

For BSE, this means that an unscrupulous manufacturer could literally take a British cow brain, crush it, dry it out, formulate it into a dietary supplement and export it to the U.S. Indeed, a letter by Dr. Scott Norton in the *New England Journal of Medicine* mentions a product available in the U.S. with 17 cow organs including brain, pituitary, and pineal gland. Due to DSHEA, the FDA is limited in what it can do. Instead of claiming that its regulatory authority over dietary supplements is adequate, as it often does publicly, the agency should be coming back to the Congress to undo the damage done by DSHEA. The best option would be to simply repeal DSHEA. In the alternative, we recommend a variety of improvements, including a mandatory adverse event reporting requirement for all dietary supplement manufacturers, mandatory risk warnings, requirements for company and product registration, and identification of the raw ingredients and the source (by country) for each of the ingredients in each product. This is, of course, a problem that goes well beyond the risk of vCJD; over 100 people have been killed by ephedra, and the agency seems essentially powerless to act. Releasing the GMP regulations for dietary supplements is necessary, but will not suffice to adequately protect American consumers from vCJD that might be caused by these products.

If the BSE agent entered the country, how might it spread?

A. Feeding Practices Since 1997, the FDA has had a ban on the feeding of mammalian parts to ruminants (e.g., cows, goats, sheep), the main route by which the BSE epidemic occurred in Britain and would be amplified in the U.S. This ban requires that manufacturers take action to prevent the commingling of two types of feed: those intended for ruminants, and those intended for nonruminants (e.g., pigs, fish, chickens which can be fed material from mammals).

FDA inspections to date provide evidence that this commingling is possible. The March 2001 FDA inspection report findings (http://www. fda.gov/cvm/index/updates/bsemar3.htm), while improved from the January 2001 findings, still shows that 14% of renderers and 13% of FDA licensed feed mills do not have adequate procedures to prevent mammalian parts from entering ruminant feed: i.e., cows could still be recycled and fed to other cows. (This is precisely what happened in the Purina Mills plant in Texas in which, purely through the voluntary admission of the company, the FDA learned that cow parts had entered cow feed. One thousand, two hundred and twenty-two cows had to be removed from the food chain.) Moreover, 23% of renderers and 63% of FDA-licensed feed mills have still not been inspected for compliance with the feed restrictions and some 6,000 to 8,000 feed mills are not even required to register with the FDA. Of the 1,829 non-FDA licensed feed mills that handle material prohibited from use in ruminant feed, 18% do not have adequate procedures to prevent the recycling of mammalian parts as feed for ruminants. If the industry does not come into better compliance with the mammal-to-ruminant ban, the FDA should consider whether a mammal-to-mammal ban is justified.

Current USDA procedures permit deer and elk from a herd with a proven case of CWD to enter the food chain.

In addition, the FDA feed ban contains an exemption that should be ended. Despite U.S. Department of Agriculture (USDA) objections, the FDA permits the feeding of so-called plate waste (leftover food that has been prepared and/or served to humans) in feed for ruminants. The European Union, Canada and Mexico have banned such practices and so should we.

Finally, there is the issue of Chronic Wasting Disease (CWD), a Transmissible Spongiform Encephalopathy (TSE) of wild and captive elk and deer. While there exists no evidence that humans have become infected from eating deer or elk, current USDA procedures permit deer and elk from a herd with a proven case of CWD to enter the food chain. The problem is that deer and elk are exempt from the USDA's Meat Inspection Act, under which the packer has the burden of demonstrating the safety of his or her product. Instead, deer and elk would have to be restricted under the FDA's Food, Drug and Cosmetic Act, which places the burden upon the agency to demonstrate potential harm and provides no funds to compensate farmers if their herd is seized. This creates an incentive for farmers not to be forthcoming about CWD in their herds. This could be addressed either by a specific regulation excluding CWD-affected herds from the food chain and providing for compensation for the rancher or by bringing deer and elk under the Meat Inspection Act, which does provide for compensation.

B. Meat Processing The processes of slaughtering and processing are not, by their nature, extremely precise ones. Infectious material from the most infectious parts of the cow, the brain and spinal cord, may spread to other parts of the animal.

Pneumatic stunning devices, which stun the animal prior to slaughter by injecting a bolt and compressed air into the head, have been shown to spread potentially infectious brain tissue to other parts of the body. Although the industry appears to be reducing its use of pneumatic stunning devices, this should be given the force of federal regulation and banned. These devices are now banned for use in cattle in Europe.

European countries require that the brain and spinal cord be removed carefully in the slaughtering process. However, in the United States, processes vary widely and are not effectively regulated. We therefore support a regulation that would require the removal of the brain and spinal cord before further processing, since these organs contain the highest levels of infectious material.

Two other meat processing methods have also come under scrutiny. In one, mechanically separated product (MSP), bones with attached muscle are crushed and pushed through an extruder to create a paste. Bone fragments are removed by a sieve-like mechanism. Both spinal cord and dorsal root ganglia (nerve tissue next to the vertebrae), which have demonstrable BSE infectivity, can enter MSP. In the other processing method, advanced meat recovery (AMR), muscle fragments are also removed from bone; this material can become part of ground beef. Early AMR machines used a belt to shave meat off bones, but later AMR machines use a "bone press" that differs from MSP only in degree. While MSP inherently involves the crushing of bones and is thus more likely to introduce nerve tissue into the product than AMR, 1997 USDA inspection records obtained by the Government Accountability Project through the Freedom of Information Act clearly demonstrate that spinal cord can be part of the material generated by AMR. Four of 34 AMR samples sent by USDA inspectors to a USDA laboratory because they were suspected of containing spinal cord tissue turned out to actually contain central nervous system tissue. It is possible that AMR machines could be redesigned to minimize the probability of crushing bones and thus including spinal cord. The USDA began such a rulemaking procedure three years ago, but the rule has still not been finalized. To prevent vCJD, we therefore support a ban on the production of MSP from vertebrae and the issuance of a final rule for better-designed AMR processes that would prevent the inclusion of spinal cord.

Is the U.S. doing enough testing to detect the disease?

To date, the U.S. surveillance efforts for BSE have been quite inadequate. Only 11,954 cow brains had been examined by the USDA in the ten-year span ending in 2000. (Some 40 million cattle are slaughtered annually in the U.S.) By comparison, France, a country which, importantly, has a proven BSE epidemic, is now testing about 20,000 brains per week.

Under current USDA procedures, all cows with neurological symptoms are supposed to be tested for BSE and, regardless of the result, excluded from the food chain. Cows that are unable to ambulate, so-called downer cows, are only occasionally tested. The USDA did not begin testing downer cows until 1993 but has now increased such testing to about 1,900 in 2000 (http://www.aphis.usda.gov/oa/bse/bsesurvey.html). This represents about 1% of all downer cows brought to slaughter in the U.S. The USDA has promised to increase such testing to 5,000 per year in 2001, a move we fully support. Testing of healthy cows does not seem justified in the U.S. at present as the prevalence of disease would most certainly be lower than in downer cows or those with neurological symptoms. . . .

To date, U.S. surveillance efforts for BSE have been quite inadequate.

Testing for the presence of BSE in cow brain can be very time-consuming. However, while three rapid tests for BSE are on the market in Europe, none are on the market in the U.S. It is imperative that these tests be evaluated by the FDA and that test performance characteristics be made public.

Surveillance for human CJD and vCJD is coordinated through the Centers for Disease Control and the National Prion Disease Pathology Surveillance Center at Case Western Reserve University. The Center has examined the brains of about 300 patients with CJD in the past four years. This represents an estimated 39% of patients with CJD in 2000, whereas in Germany and Britain the brains of almost all patients with CJD are examined by pathologists. Canada has recently revamped its surveillance system and provides much more funding for such efforts than does the U.S.

The U.S. government also needs to do more to increase the overall hospital autopsy rate in this country, which has declined from over 40% after World War II to under 10% at present, as well as to increase the rate of examination of brain material specifically. Currently, hospitals and families bear the costs of autopsies, including transportation costs; they should be reimbursed for these costs. The government should also consider creating a network of regional pathology centers to do brain examinations for CJD and needs to do more to contact all neurologists to inform them of the current surveillance system.

Are there medical practices that might transmit BSE and vCJD?

In weighing whether products that are transfused or transplanted into humans should be restricted, the essential questions are: 1. What is the probability of transmission of infection?; 2. Are there suitable alternatives to the material?; and 3. Would the restriction of the material produce a shortage of a vital medical product?

While there has never been a documented case of CJD or vCJD transmitted by blood transfusion, the agent is present in white blood cells (inevitably present to some extent in even red blood cell transfusions) and, in an experiment, a sheep was recently infected by transfusion from a cow with BSE. In 1999, the FDA's TSE Advisory Committee recommended a ban on blood donations from potential donors who had spent more than a total of six months in Britain between 1980 and 1996. The Committee determined that the impact on the blood supply would be manageable and data collected since the restriction on British donors confirm that the supply of blood remained stable after the ban was enacted. In January 2001, with cases of vCJD in France and of BSE in Europe mounting, the Committee extended this recommendation to include France, Portugal and Ireland, although with a 10-year cumulative residency requirement, since BSE and vCJD case rates are lower in those countries than in Britain. The FDA should adopt the Committee's recommendation.

For the public to be adequately protected [against mad cow disease], government will have to take forceful action . . . and not simply depend upon voluntary actions by industry.

Similar travel restrictions should be placed on cadaveric cornea donors, especially because as many as three cases of CJD due to corneal transplantation have been documented. Due to the existing shortages of other transplantable organs such as heart and bone marrow, and the failure to document CJD transmission associated with their transplantation, a travel restriction on such organ donors is not justified. On the other hand, because the U.S. is a net exporter of cornea, we are not concerned that there would be a shortage of cornea were a travel restriction to be implemented.

The issue of vaccines

In 1993, the FDA wrote to the manufacturers of FDA regulated products and in a voluntary Guidance instructed manufacturers to no longer source materials for their products from BSE-affected countries. It repeated the admonition in 1996. Nonetheless, at least six manufacturers simply ignored the Guidance, which does not have the force of a regulation, and continued to source bovine materials for the production of vaccines from BSE-affected countries. The FDA only learnt that its recommendation had been disregarded in early 2000. By then, millions of doses of vaccines such as polio and diphtheria, tetanus, and pertussis (DTP) were injected into Americans, including small children. At a TSE Advisory Committee meeting in July 2000, Committee members agreed that the risk of disease transmission through these vaccines is extremely small and that there is no evidence that vCJD has been spread through this route. Nonetheless, this event was a reminder of the dangers presented by agencies that fail to regulate and industries that act in arrogant disregard of the government.

The lesson of the vaccine debacle applies more broadly to our efforts to reduce the risks of BSE and vCJD: for the public to be adequately protected, government will have to take forceful action—regulations, not guidelines—and not simply depend upon voluntary actions by industry.

3

The Threat of Mad Cow Disease in the United States Has Been Exaggerated

Abigail Trafford

Abigail Trafford is a health columnist for the Washington Post.

The risk of contracting mad cow disease in the United States is minimal. Americans are more likely to contract bacterial types of food-borne illnesses, such as *Listeriosis* or *Salmonella*, than they are mad cow disease. Even if a cow—the main transmitter of the disease—did become sick, officials would isolate the animal long before it could become part of the food chain and a risk to humans. People need to put the potential risk from mad cow disease in perspective and not allow irrational fear to cloud their judgment about whether or not to continue to eat beef.

The man at a dinner party leans over and asks: "Are you worried about 'mad cow' disease? Should we stop eating steak?"

I laugh. Earth to Chicken Little! The sky is not falling on steak. Not here, anyway. Of all the things to worry about, getting mad cow disease from a nice juicy filet mignon is not one of them. Not yet, anyway.

I go through the obvious arguments. Not a single case has occurred in the United States in man or beast. [In December 2003 a cow in Washington state was diagnosed with mad cow disease.] Precautions are in place to prevent the disease from spreading to this country. Feed made from certain animals—the suspected culprit in Europe—is prohibited here. Beef and beef products from affected countries are banned. Even in Europe, fewer than 100 people have succumbed to the strange malady since the outbreak began four years ago [1998]. Those cases have been confined to Britain, Ireland and France where—statistically speaking—people are five times more likely to be killed by a bolt of lightning than by mad cow disease.

If you're going to worry about what you eat, there are bigger food-borne killers. For starters, listeriosis (from contaminated meats, dairy products, raw vegetables) and salmonella (from contaminated raw eggs) each cause 500 deaths a year in this country. *E. coli*, which is most associated with eating contaminated ground beef, kills 61 people a year. Why worry about something that hasn't killed anybody in this country?

The expression on the dinner guest's face goes from polite disagreement to pity. I must sound like a victim of *"Animal Farm"* propaganda from the agri-medical establishment. He doesn't believe a reassuring word I've said.

Why should he? Europe is in a panic over mad cow disease. Overall consumption of beef dropped 27 percent from October to December [of 2000]. The cattle industry has been crushed and governments are shaken. Instead of promoting the national staple of *le steak et pommes frites*, French farmers are throwing stones at their prime minister.

Fear of mad cow disease is unfounded

The fear is spreading to these shores: Cattle in Texas quarantined after eating bone meal. Elk in Oklahoma diagnosed with a chronic wasting disease. Suspect mad cow candy on sale in New York City.

Mamba fruit chew, banned in Poland, is made with a beef-based gelatin produced in Germany, where about 20 cows have been found to be infected with bovine spongiform encephalopathy (BSE), the scientific name for mad cow disease. In the ensuing public-relations meltdown, the company announced it would switch from beef gelatin to vegetable starch.

Of all the things to worry about, getting mad cow disease from a nice juicy filet mignon is not one of them.

Call that Mad Cow Panic Syndrome (MCPS). Tests have shown that the disease cannot be transmitted in gelatin, even from infected cattle, says George Gray, director of the program for food safety and agriculture at the Harvard School of Public Health's Center for Risk Analysis in Boston. "It's a nonissue," he says. "This situation takes on a life of its own."

The perception of risk is wildly out of proportion to the actual risk. "When I have a hamburger, I worry much more about *E. coli* than a chance of BSE," Gray says. Even if an animal in the United States shows up sick one day, there would be no immediate threat to people. Tightened surveillance would prevent the spread to other animals and keep the infected animal from reaching the human food chain. "It's not going to be a big public health risk," Gray continues. But if that day comes, he adds, "we'll go bonkers."

People fear mysterious diseases

Mad cow bonkers. All of us from Henny Penny to Goosey Loosey have a hard time dealing with risks. Certain kinds of hazards, no matter how rare, grab our imagination so that we fear the worst. They usually share these characteristics:

Mysterious. Just what causes mad cow disease is not known. The prime suspect is a prion, an aberrant protein that attacks the central nervous system. Scientists are used to bacteria and viruses, but prions are a new kind of infectious agent. The theory is that herds in Britain were infected from contaminated bone meal. BSE crossed from animals to people, causing a variant of the rare degenerative brain disorder called Creutzfeldt-Jakob disease. There is no evidence, points out Harvard's Gray, that the prions get into muscle meat—in other words, into steak. Greatest concern is focused on brain and bones and mixed meats such as sausage.

Lethal. The disease is horrible and invariably fatal. About 300 Americans die of the classic form of Creutzfeldt-Jakob disease a year, which strikes seemingly at random. There is no effective treatment. With listeriosis, for example, an estimated 2,500 Americans get very sick, but they can be treated with antibiotics and most of them recover. Mad cow disease is a death sentence, and victims are generally younger than those who succumb to the classic form of the brain malady.

Unpredictable. The infection in cattle peaked in 1993. Since then, Britain has slaughtered infected herds and tested cattle to make sure they are healthy. Last year [2000], the European Union banned the use of remnant parts mammal feed to reduce the chances of contamination. At the same time, the incubation period in people for this disease could be anywhere from two to 20 years. Health officials don't know if the number of cases will level off. Or whether the current toll represents the tip of an epidemic iceberg of many more people who harbor the infection. "We don't know how many people are infected. We don't know the size of the risk," says psychologist Baruch Fischhoff of Carnegie Mellon University.

To date, mad cow disease is not a crisis in public health; but it's becoming a crisis in public trust.

There is not a lot people can do to reduce their personal risk. You can avoid lightning by staying indoors in a thunderstorm (about 300 deaths in the United States annually) and prevent head injuries on a bicycle by wearing a helmet (about 800 deaths a year). You can avoid salmonella by cooking eggs and listeriosis by sticking to pasteurized cheese.

But it's hard to control your exposure to all the theoretically possible avenues to mad cow disease—even when there is no evidence of a problem. Just last week [early February 2001], the headlines screeched that five major drug companies had used ingredients from cattle in affected European countries to manufacture vaccines given to millions of American children—contrary to recommendations of the FDA. Animal-based gelatin is also used in supplements with little government oversight.

The prions are falling! In a world of medical globalism, neither diseases nor drugs recognize national boundaries. To date, mad cow disease is not a crisis in public health; but it's becoming a crisis in public trust.

4

America's Food Supply Is Threatened by Terrorism

Katrina Woznicki

Katrina Woznicki is a science writer for United Press International, a worldwide news service.

The September 11, 2001, terrorist attacks put every aspect of American life in jeopardy, including the safety of the nation's food supply. Within two weeks of the attacks, the Food and Drug Administration, Centers for Disease Control and Prevention (CDC), Environmental Protection Agency, U.S. Department of Agriculture, and National Food Processors Association created a food security plan. They developed simple recommendations to help protect the nation's food supply. For example, they encourage food companies to light property to discourage break-ins, lock up food products, and limit access to food products to employees. Further, the CDC is ready to respond immediately to identify and isolate any outbreaks of food-borne illness should they occur.

A mericans already know what it is like to fear lethal anthrax lurking in their mail, but when they go to take a bite out of a sandwich or sit down to a family dinner, how can they be sure they are not about to ingest these deadly microorganisms?

Since [the September 11, 2001, terrorist attacks], bioterrorism became the federal government's number one priority. The subject includes food security—protecting the nation's food supply from a bioterrorism attack.

"I don't think a year ago we were very concerned about possibilities of food terrorism," Dr. Charles Sizer, director of the National Center for Food Safety and Technology in Chicago, Ill. told United Press International (UPI). "This is going to be a long-term, evolving, type of issue. It's a new reality that we have live to with."

Not since 1984 when cult followers of an Indian guru used *salmonella* as a weapon to spike salad bars at 10 restaurants in an Oregon town have Americans even been worried about deliberate food contamination with bacteria. The Oregon case sickened 750 people.

Eighteen years later, advanced technology and a decentralized food supply make it possible for terrorists to contaminate the U.S. food supply and sicken or even kill thousands of citizens.

For example, could a cow be intentionally contaminated with bovine spongiform encephalopathy or mad cow's disease and slipped into the nation's meat supply? On April 22, [2002,] Food and Drug Administration Deputy Commissioner Lester M. Crawford told the Consumer Federation of America, "That is a threat we're watching very closely."

Or could fresh produce be laced with harmful microbes? Although FDA declined to provide possible scenarios it's preparing for—a spokesperson told UPI, "It is FDA's policy not to discuss potential threats"—experts say no one knows what could happen so it is best to be prepared for anything.

"I don't think we know the worst possible case," said Helen Jensen, a member of the National Research Committee, part of the National Academy of Sciences that helped review food security protocol and an economics professor at Iowa State University in Ames, Iowa. "Based on our experience in the last six months, we're seeing things we never expected to see."

To respond to this potential threat, FDA is expected to use $98 million of its $1.727 billion proposed budget for Fiscal Year 2003 specifically for food security.

Since [the September 11, 2001, terrorist attacks], bioterrorism became the federal government's number one priority. The subject includes . . . protecting the nation's food supply from a bioterrorism attack.

Meanwhile, FDA has wasted no time. Since January 10, [2002,] it already has hired 250 food safety inspectors whose jobs it will be to monitor the food distribution process, including checking every single step in food's progress from the farm to someone's dinner plate.

"FDA has been authorized to hire approximately 650 new field personnel" for inspections, Robert E. Brackett, food safety director of the FDA's Center for Food Safety and Applied Nutrition, told UPI. "Although the recent security concerns have accelerated hiring plans, it has been recognized for years that FDA's food inspection capacity needs to be enhanced as part of its normal food safety effort."

These inspectors will be responsible for going through food safety checklists, for both imported and domestic products, to ensure food never gets into the wrong hands or deviates from its scheduled distribution. Random screenings for food pathogens also will be conducted, explained Rhona Applebaum, executive vice president for scientific and regulatory affairs for the National Food Processors Association (NFPA), an organization working closely with FDA on food security.

Preventing food terrorism from the top down

Most Americans do not know where their food comes from because the source of the nation's food supply is so varied and vast. "It's no longer like you know the butcher that's in your local community," Jensen said. This makes coordinating food terrorism prevention an effort starting at the federal level and trickling all the way down to the small farmer or restaurant chain.

Experts . . . cannot even forecast the likelihood of a terrorism attack in food. They just know that after Sept. 11, the country needs to be on guard all the time.

Applebaum said her office contacted FDA Sept. 12, [2001,] about co-ordinating a food security protection plan. The Washington, D.C.–based NFPA met with not only FDA, but also the Centers for Disease Control and Prevention [CDC], the Environmental Protection Agency and the U.S. Department of Agriculture to design guidelines for those involved in the American food chain, including restaurants and food suppliers and distributors big and small. All comprise the Security for Food Alliance, formally created two weeks after the terrorist attacks.

Although some food companies have boosted their surveillance technology to better monitor the facility and employees, the guidelines involve "very low technology," Sizer said.

"Light it, lock it and limit access to it," Applebaum said. Meaning: light the property to reduce the chance of break-ins, lock up the food products, and know the personnel working at the food facility and limit the people with access to the product.

"What you want to make sure you do whether it's a restaurant or a processing plant is that you want to make sure you have some information on the people working for you," Applebaum explained. This can be a challenge, particularly in low-paying restaurants or plants where employee turnover can be high. But Applebaum said if security checklists are fully followed, the guidelines work.

"The more hurdles we put between a person focused on doing evil and the consumer, the less likely it would be for a major (terrorism) event," Applebaum said.

The guidelines may seem simple, but they were designed to allow smaller companies with smaller budgets to be able to participate in national food security efforts.

The CDC is vital

How would federal officials be able to discern a foodborne illness outbreak from a terrorist attack?

"FDA relies upon its sister agency, the Centers for Disease Control and Prevention, and similar state agencies for surveillance and outbreak detection," Brackett said. "Epidemiologists in these agencies are trained to analyze disease patterns and would be the first to detect the source and cause of an outbreak."

Experts concede it might not be possible to know the difference between the two scenarios immediately, but that doesn't affect the initial response, which is to remove contaminated food from the food supply immediately and isolate those who have been sickened, especially if the pathogen is contagious. The fact that responding to a food bioterrorism attack would be similar to responding to a foodborne illness outbreak works in public health officials' favor.

"We have decades of experiences and literally daily experience in dealing with this," said Dr. Jeremy Sobel, a medical epidemiologist with CDC in Atlanta.

When it comes to food bioterrorism, communication is key. CDC already has in place a technologically sophisticated surveillance system allowing real-time electronic correspondence connecting CDC headquarters, state health departments and other local health departments so any foodborne illness or attack can be quickly identified, tracked, quarantined and followed throughout the country.

"In the case of bioterrorism," Sobel explained, this electronic network is crucial in "identifying the perpetrator and getting him off the market too."

CDC also has a genetic fingerprinting system at all state health departments based on collections of previous foodborne pathogens taken from patient and food samples. Having this database of food microbes on hand helps epidemiologists quickly identify any genetic differences in food contaminants.

This could help scientists distinguish an attack from an outbreak and rapidly detect if contaminants have a common source should simultaneous multiple attacks or outbreaks occur throughout the U.S.

Experts said they cannot even forecast the likelihood of a bioterrorism attack in food. They just know that after Sept. 11, the country needs to be on guard all the time.

"We know it's a possibility," Applebaum said. "We don't know what the probability is."

5

Food-Borne Illnesses Are Declining in the United States

Centers for Disease Control and Prevention

The Centers for Disease Control and Prevention (CDC) is part of the U.S. Department of Health and Human Services. It is the federal agency responsible for protecting the health and safety of Americans.

Salmonella and Campylobacter, two of the most common causes of food-borne illness in the United States, have declined significantly in recent years. A science-based inspection system of meat and poultry processing plants is credited with the decrease in disease. The system, Pathogen Reduction and Hazard Analysis and Critical Control Point (HACCP), requires that processing plants develop preventative controls and meet pathogen reduction performance standards for Salmonella. Periodic inspection ensures that plants meet these standards.

The Department of Health and Human Services today released preliminary data from the Centers for Disease Control and Prevention (CDC) that show a decline in the overall incidence of *Salmonella* and *Campylobacter* infections, two of the most common causes of foodborne disease in the United States. The data come from the Foodborne Diseases Active Surveillance Network (FoodNet).

"These new findings are encouraging and show that our intensified fight against foodborne illness is paying off," said HHS Secretary Donna E. Shalala. "However, we still have work to do. Foodborne disease remains a substantial public health burden that affects millions of people every year. I urge Congress to support our efforts to expand food safety programs throughout the Department."

The data show a 13 percent decline in the number of *Salmonella* infections between 1996 and 1998 and a 44 percent drop in the incidence of *Salmonella* enteritidis, a subtype of *Salmonella* infection associated with egg contamination that has been a major food safety problem since the

Centers for Disease Control and Prevention, *"Salmonella* and *Campylobacter* Illnesses on the Decline," www.cdc.gov, March 11, 1999.

1980s. The data also indicate a 15 percent decline between 1997–1998 in the number of illnesses caused by *Campylobacter*, the most common bacterial foodborne pathogen in the United States. The preliminary findings were collected from five FoodNet sites in California, Georgia, Connecticut, Minnesota, and Oregon and published in the March 12 issue of *Morbidity and Mortality Weekly Report (MMWR)*.

The data show a 13 percent decline in the number of Salmonella *infections between 1996 and 1998.*

"The Administration's new, science-based inspection system requires meat and poultry plants to take steps to prevent contamination by *Salmonella* and other potentially dangerous pathogens," said Agriculture Secretary Dan Glickman. "Our new system has resulted in a sharp decrease in *Salmonella* contamination of raw meat and poultry and, we believe, contributed to this decline in foodborne illnesses."

FoodNet data can be used to document the effectiveness of new food safety control measures such as USDA's [U.S. Department of Agriculture] Pathogen Reduction and Hazard Analysis and Critical Control Points (HACCP) Rule as well as HACCP programs undertaken by the Food and Drug Administration (FDA) for seafood and other food products.

Under the HACCP system, plants must develop a system of preventive controls and meet pathogen reduction performance standards for *Salmonella* set by USDA. Testing occurs to ensure that plants are meeting these tough standards.

Increased prevention efforts are working

"These reported declines in foodborne disease are encouraging and suggest that the stepped up prevention efforts of the USDA and the FDA may be working," said CDC director Dr. Jeffrey Koplan. "However, the reasons for these declines are not fully understood and more study is needed."

The incidence of *E. coli* 0157:H7 went from 2.7 cases per 100,000 population in 1996 to 2.3 in 1997 and then up to 2.8 per 100,000 in 1998. The fluctuation could be a normal variation. CDC continues to gather data about which specific foods caused the illnesses; however, previous studies have linked *E. Coli* infection to milk, drinking water, roast or ground beef, apple cider, lettuce and venison, among other foods, and even to swimming in pools and lakes.

FoodNet is a joint effort by HHS, the USDA, and state health departments to capture a more accurate and complete picture of trends in the occurrence of foodborne illness. Within HHS, the network involves the CDC and the FDA.

At FoodNet sites, public health officials frequently contact microbiology laboratories and other data sources for illness that may be caused by different foodborne pathogens on an active, ongoing basis using standardized data collection methods. Each case is reviewed and strains of the organisms are collected and analyzed. Special case control studies are conducted in order to identify the major risk factors for disease. Data are then electronically submitted to CDC for analysis.

FoodNet sites began collecting data in 1996. Currently sites are located in California, Connecticut, Georgia, Maryland, Minnesota, New York, and Oregon. The total population of these sites is 20.5 million (7.7% of the total U.S. population). Additional FoodNet sites will be added to the program; Tennessee is scheduled to begin collecting data in 1999.

CDC is currently using incidence and community survey data from FoodNet as well as other data sources to improve the estimates of total foodborne illness in the United States. These estimates, soon to be published, will provide the best information to date on the burden of food-borne disease in the United States.

6

Food-Borne Illnesses Are a Threat to Europe

World Health Organization

The World Health Organization is the United Nations' specialized agency for health.

Food-borne illnesses have increased markedly in eastern and western Europe in the past decade. As many as one person in three in industrialized countries may be affected by food-borne diseases every year. Most illness is bacterial, caused by *Salmonella* and *Campylobacter* pathogens, or the result of contamination from chemical sources, such as lead or dioxin. Differences in national food safety and quality policies across Europe make it difficult to uniformly protect the health and well-being of consumers in the region. All countries should have science-based risk assessment and management systems in place to minimize the dangers posed by food-borne illnesses.

Food safety and quality need to be improved in all European countries because foodborne diseases have increased considerably in the region in the past decade, the UN Food and Agriculture Organization (FAO) and the World Health Organization (WHO) said in a joint statement issued today. On the rise in particular are diseases from microbiological hazards such as *Salmonella* and *Campylobacter* and cases of foods contaminated by chemical hazards, such as dioxin, lead and cadmium, according to the two UN agencies.

The statement was issued on the opening day [February 25, 2002] of the *First Pan-European Conference on Food Safety and Quality* in Budapest [Hungary]. Food safety experts from more than 40 countries, including food producers and consumers' associations from Western, Central and Eastern Europe and other countries in transition are meeting in Budapest to discuss how to improve food safety and strengthen consumer confidence after recent food scares.

The meeting is jointly organized by FAO and WHO. It is co-sponsored by the European Community and some FAO/WHO member countries.

"While food has never been safer than it is today in Europe, this should not lead us to complacency. Better monitoring systems are revealing more and more cases of food-borne illness. The number of people suffering from food-borne diseases or even die from them is still far too high," said Hartwig de Haen, FAO Assistant Director-General.

"WHO estimates that, worldwide, thousands of millions of cases of food-borne disease occur every year. As many as one person in three in industrialized countries may be affected by foodborne illness each year, resulting in human suffering and economic losses running into billions of US dollars. Particularly at risk are children, pregnant women, the sick, the poor and the elderly," said Dr David Nabarro, WHO Executive Director.

Food safety and quality need to be improved in all European countries because foodborne diseases have increased considerably in the region in the past decade.

"The consumer has the right to safe food in all European countries. Food safety 'from farm to fork' needs to be ensured throughout the region. To save costs and prevent contamination, food safety must begin with good agricultural practices," de Haen added.

National policies and regulations on food safety and quality are still very diverse in Europe, according to de Haen. "Food safety control systems in Central and Eastern Europe as well as in Central Asian Republics are very different from the EU [European Union], and also vary among each other. Europe is certainly not aiming for a single standard diet. The challenge is: harmonisation in diversity. We need to bring different food safety and quality policies across Europe closer together to protect the health and well-being of consumers. Different food safety systems need to become comparable and fully transparent."

National and international agencies must work together

"Problems with food safety over the last decades have been aggravated by lack of collaboration between different authorities at the national level. WHO, together with FAO and our Member States are working hard to develop new, evidence-based, preventative strategies to lower risk of disease. This work focuses on the whole food production chain. We promote a dialogue with consumers. We encourage interdisciplinary collaboration all the way from farm to table. Different authorities at the national level and different international organizations will have to work together and coordinate their efforts for this to work," noted Nabarro.

Salmonella is still the most frequently reported causal agent of foodborne disease outbreaks in East and West European countries, according to FAO/WHO. Outbreaks occur in private homes and in mass catering kitchens in restaurants, cafeterias, catering services, schools, kindergartens and hospitals.

In addition, *Campylobacter* is currently the most commonly reported gastrointestinal pathogen in many countries, including Denmark, Finland, Iceland, Ireland, the Netherlands, Norway, Sweden, Switzerland and the United Kingdom. Campylobacteriosis is a bacterial infection that affects the intestinal tract.

The contamination of food by chemical hazards is another major public health concern. In Central and Eastern Europe food contamination arises largely from industrial contamination of air, soil and water. One of the hot spots is the Aral Sea area. For almost 30 years the use of water for irrigation of cotton monoculture and the heavy use of insecticides, pesticides and herbicides has created a critical situation for the health of the local population.

FAO/WHO recommended that all countries have science-based risk assessment and management systems in place to deal with microbiological and chemical hazards in food. In some countries, infrastructure needs to be strengthened to achieve a higher level of protection. "Agriculture and health institutions must work together to ensure food safety," de Haen said.

Currently FAO and WHO are performing a number of microbiological risk assessments, the first ever to be performed at the international level. The food-pathogen combinations that have been identified through various expert consultations as deserving immediate attention are *Listeria* in ready-to-eat foods, *Campylobacter* in poultry, *Vibrio* in seafood, and *Salmonella* in eggs and poultry. "These risk assessments will provide templates for Member States to adapt them to their national situation and to assist them in addressing the threats of these pathogens in the most efficient way," Nabarro said.

FAO and WHO stressed the many advantages of safer and high quality food. "Safer food means lower incidence of foodborne diseases, lower public health costs, fewer barriers to international trade, lower productivity losses and better competitiveness."

7

Food-Borne Illnesses
Are Costly

Economic Research Service

The Economic Research Service (ERS) is the main source of economic information and research from the U.S. Department of Agriculture. The mission of ERS is to inform and enhance public and private decision making on economic and policy issues related to agriculture, food, natural resources, and rural development.

Costs associated with food-borne illnesses in the United States are estimated to be about $6.9 billion annually. These estimates include medical costs, productivity losses from missed work, and an estimate of the value of premature death. In addition to causing immediate symptoms, food-borne diseases often result in chronic illnesses that affect the joints, nervous system, kidneys, or heart, and lead to additional lifelong medical costs or premature death.

F oodborne diseases are caused by ingesting bacteria, fungi, parasites, or viruses through contaminated food or water, or through person-to-person contact. The Centers for Disease Control and Prevention (CDC) estimates that foodborne diseases cause approximately 76 million illnesses, 325,000 hospitalizations, and 5,000 deaths in the United States each year. ERS has estimated the annual U.S. economic costs incurred for the major bacterial pathogens: *Escherichia coli* O157 and other STECs [Shiga toxin-producing *Escherichia coli*] (an associated hemolytic uremic syndrome), *Campylobacter* (an associated Guillain-Barré syndrome), *Listeria monocytogenes*, and *Salmonella*. In addition, ERS has developed outcome trees for the illnesses caused by those pathogens, showing the costs incurred and the number of cases by the severity of disease: no physician visit, hospitalization, premature death, and chronic complications.

In 2000, ERS estimated that the costs associated with five major pathogens amount to at least $6.9 billion annually. The cost estimate includes medical costs, productivity losses from missed work, and an estimate of the value of premature death that takes into account the age distribution of those taken ill. The estimate excludes travel costs in obtaining

Economic Research Service, "Economics of Foodborne Disease: Overview," www.ers.usda.gov, February 7, 2003.

medical care, lost leisure time, and so forth. Estimates for *Salmonella* were updated in 2003.

ERS also evaluated the pros and cons of the two principal methods of estimating the monetary benefits of reducing foodborne diseases: cost-of-illness and willingness-to-pay. In addition, ERS looked at the pros and cons of three other methods (risk-risk analysis, health-health analysis, and cost-effectiveness analysis) that try to avoid assigning a monetary value to human life and health.

Foodborne diseases are acute and chronic

Pathogens are disease-causing microorganisms that include bacteria, fungi, parasites, and viruses. Most cases of foodborne illnesses are classified as "acute." These are usually self-limiting and of short duration, although they can range from mild to severe. Gastrointestinal problems and vomiting are common acute symptoms of many foodborne illnesses. Deaths from acute foodborne illnesses, while rare, are more likely to occur in the very young, the elderly, or patients with compromised immune systems (such as those suffering from AIDS or cancer). However, the U.S. Food and Drug Administration (FDA) estimates that 2 to 3 percent of all acute cases develop secondary long-term illnesses, called "chronic sequellae."

Chronic sequellae of foodborne illness can occur in any part of the body and subsequently affect the joints, nervous system, kidneys, or heart. These chronic illnesses may afflict the patients for the remainder of their lives or result in premature death. For example, *Campylobacter* infections are estimated to be responsible for 20 to 40 percent of Guillain-Barré syndrome (GBS) cases (a major cause of paralysis unrelated to trauma) in the United States. About 1.5 percent of *E. coli* O157 disease patients develop hemolytic uremic syndrome (HUS), which usually involves red blood cell destruction, kidney failure, and neurological complications, such as seizures and strokes.

Actions by the food industry, consumers, and the public health sector influence how food is produced, marketed, prepared, and consumed. These actions influence the probability that a food item contains pathogens. People who consume contaminated food have some probability of becoming ill. Foodborne illness generates costs that are borne by the food industry, households whose members become ill, and/or the public health sector.

Foodborne diseases cause approximately 76 million illnesses, 325,000 hospitalizations, and 5,000 deaths in the United States each year.

ERS estimates of the costs of foodborne disease are limited to estimating the impact on households. Thus, ERS is underestimating the impact of foodborne illness on society. In fact, we estimate only the medical costs, productivity losses, and the value associated with premature death for a selected number of microbial foodborne health risks. The ERS cost estimates undervalue the household's cost of foodborne illness because some costs are omitted, such as travel to obtain medical care, time lost from work caring for sick children, lost leisure time, pain and suffering, and the costs of certain other chronic complications, such as reactive arthritis in the case of *Salmonella*.

ERS cost estimates are calculated from the number of acute and chronic foodborne-illness cases and deaths caused by each pathogen each year. These costs include medical costs, lost productivity costs, other ill-ness-specific costs (such as special education and residential-care costs), and an estimate of the value of premature deaths.

Societal costs have not been estimated for the vast majority of complications associated with foodborne illnesses. The Centers for Disease Control and Prevention (CDC) estimates that out of a total of 76 million cases of foodborne disease each year in the United States, as many as 62 million cases are of unknown origin. We do, however, cover the following chronic complications in our cost estimates: GBS following *Campylobacter* infections, HUS following *E. coli* O157 infections, and chronic disability or impairment following congenital and newborn infections from *Listeria monocytogenes*.

Medical costs

For each foodborne illness, cases are generally divided into five severity levels: 1) those who do not visit a physician, 2) those who visit a physician, 3) those who are hospitalized, 4) those who developed chronic complications, and 5) those who die prematurely because of their illness.

For each severity group, medical costs are estimated for physician and hospital services, supplies, medications, and special procedures unique to treating the particular foodborne illnesses. Such costs reflect the number of days/treatments of a medical service, the average cost per service/treatment, and the number of patients receiving such service/treatment.

In 2000, ERS estimated that the costs associated with five major pathogens [causing food-borne illnesses] amount to at least $6.9 billion annually.

Beginning with estimates released in 2000, ERS cost estimates use a "labor market approach", incorporating information about the wage premiums for high-risk occupations. Cost estimates also use information about the age distribution of deaths to adjust this value to account for the age at death.

In essence, the labor market approach values the economic cost of premature deaths based on the risk premium revealed by the higher wages paid for dangerous jobs. Under this approach, the value of a statistical life equaled $6.5 million in August 2000 dollars after updating the original 1990 estimate of $5.0 million to account for inflation. The labor market approach assumes that risk preferences observed in job choices are indicative of risk preferences for food safety.

ERS modified the labor market approach by taking the age distribution of deaths from each pathogen into account, in effect treating the value of life as an annuity paid over the average U.S. life span at an interest rate of 3.0 percent. Following age-adjustment, the assumed cost of each death was five times higher for individuals who died before their first birthday than for individuals who died at age 85 or older.

Since the five microbial pathogens have different health outcomes for different age groups, adjusting for the age of death raises the cost of some foodborne illnesses and lowers the cost of others. For example, the estimated annual cost of foodborne illnesses caused by *Salmonella* decreased because over two-thirds of the deaths from salmonellosis occur among people over 65 years of age. Adjusting foodborne illness costs for *E. coli* O157 by age at time of death increased the estimate because most deaths are children under the age of five.

Productivity losses

One difficult issue is assigning a value to the productivity losses associated with individuals who become ill and are unable to return to work, or for those illnesses that result in a lifetime of disability (such as prenatal exposure to *Listeria monocytogenes*). ERS currently measures the productivity losses due to nonfatal foodborne illnesses by the value of forgone or lost wages, regardless of whether the lost wages involved a few days missed from work or a permanent disability that prevented an individual from returning to work. Using the value of lost wages for cases resulting in disability probably understates an individual's willingness to pay to avoid disability because it does not account for the value placed on avoiding pain and suffering. The willingness to pay measure derived from labor market studies that ERS uses to value a premature death is not an appropriate measure of willingness to pay to avoid disability because it measures the higher wages paid to workers to accept a higher risk of premature death, not disability. Methods have been suggested to adjust willingness to pay to reduce the risk of premature death downward to estimate willingness to pay to avoid disability, such as the approach based on measuring "Quality Adjusted Life Years" (QALY). As yet, there is no consensus among economists about how to use these methods to value willingness to pay to avoid the disability, pain, and suffering associated with foodborne illnesses. ERS's conservative estimates of the annual costs due to foodborne illnesses (particularly the chronic conditions associated with *Campylobacter*) would be substantially increased if willingness to pay to avoid disability, pain, and suffering were also taken into account.

8

Genetically Modified Food Causes Food-Borne Illnesses

Physicians and Scientists for Responsible Application of Science and Technology

Physicians and Scientists for Responsible Application of Science and Technology is an organization of professional scientists and laypeople who are concerned about the conditions that are hampering impartial comprehensive, interdisciplinary evaluations of the safety of new applications of science and technology—particularly the genetic modification of plants and animals used for food.

A considerable increase in the rate of food-borne illnesses occurring in the United States from 1994 to 1999 can be traced directly to an enormous rise in the consumption of genetically engineered (GE) foods during the same time period. One explanation for the link between an increase in food-borne illnesses and the use of GE foods is the creation of new viruses during the engineering of these foods. Because GE food plants contain virus genes that are similar to human virus genes, genetic mutations can occur creating new viruses. These new mutated viruses can cause illness in people who eat GE food. In addition, *Bacillus thuringiensis* (Bt)—common in GE food—is responsible for intestinal irritation which may cause acute as well as chronic gastrointestinal illnesses. Moreover, bacterial DNA sequences present in almost all GE foods may increase the likelihood of intestinal inflammation, as well as other inflammatory diseases such as rheumatoid arthritis. Thus, the increase in food-borne illnesses may indeed be linked to GE foods.

In [the] USA, between 1994 and 1999, the rate of illnesses caused by food has doubled for some kinds of diseases and increased tenfold for other kinds. As a comparison, the rate in Sweden in 1999 was about the same as it was in the US in 1994.

Mae-Wan Ho, director of the Institute of Science in the Society, and an expert on food biotechnology notes in a recent report that there is a very pronounced difference between Sweden and the US in one respect—

Physicians and Scientists for Responsible Application of Science and Technology, "Considerable Increase of Foodborne Diseases in the U.S.—GE a Cause?" www.psrast.org, July 9, 2003. Copyright © 2003 by Physicians and Scientists for Responsible Application of Science and Technology. Reproduced by permission.

the rate of virus-caused illnesses. While in Sweden, viruses were the cause in only 9% of the cases, they were so in 80% of the cases in the USA.

The reason for this increase is unknown. But Mae-Wan Ho points out that *the use of genetically engineered foods has increased enormously in the US since 1994.* By comparison, in Sweden, almost no GE [genetically engineered] foods were used in 1999.

GE crops can generate new viruses

Ho suspects that a possible reason might be that GE foods may give rise to new viruses. This has been well established scientifically (even the biotech firm Monsanto has acknowledged this). The reason is that every cell in GE plants contains parts of virus genes that can combine with the genes of infecting viruses. In a very large proportion of GE crop varieties, the virus genes come from a virus (Cauliflower Mosaic Virus—CaMV) related to human viruses. Therefore some scientists have warned that GE plants may give rise to new human viruses.

New bacterial pathogens?

Ho has warned that so called vector DNA used in all GE crops may also be a culprit. This DNA comes from virus and bacteria and facilitates the combination of genes of unrelated species. Thereby it might promote the emergence of new bacteria.

How GE foods cause illness

We agree that the large scale cultivation of GE crops brings with it a definite risk for the emergence of new viruses. But if this were the cause of a major part of foodborne disease increase, it should also have caused a considerable increase of virus diseases affecting other organs. We are not aware that this has happened. So we assume that, if new viruses have contributed to the increase of foodborne diseases, it is likely to be to a minor extent.

The large scale cultivation of GE crops brings with it a definite risk for the emergence of new viruses.

We propose another explanation how GE foods might be the cause. It is based on the remarkable fact that 82% of the foodborne diseases and 25% of the death cases were caused by "unknown pathogens" in the American study that Ho refers to.

In addition, in practical medicine, the diagnosis of "virus GE disorder" mostly occurs through exclusion as it is costly and not useful to detect all the potential viral pathogens (as there is no specific therapy for viral diseases, specific diagnosis is of no help). So when, in a case of pronounced diarrhoic disease, the common pathogens, like *salmonella, shigella* etc., have been excluded, it is often assumed that the disease is viral.

We suggest that part of the foodborne diseases of unknown origin as well as of the "virus disorders" may perhaps have been caused by GE foods in two possible ways:

1. By a known toxin common in genetically engineered food. It is the *Bacillus thuringiensis* (Bt) toxin.
2. By bacterial DNA used for genetic engineering in almost all GE foods.

1. Major GE crops have been genetically engineered to produce the Bt toxin for its insecticidal ability.

Professor Joe Cummins has recently pointed out that an Egyptian study indicates that the Bt toxin causes intestinal irritation which may cause acute as well as chronic gastrointestinal illness. This study found that mice, fed with genetically engineered potatoes, developed significant intestinal changes indicating an irritative effect of the toxin.

We suggest that part of the foodborne diseases of unknown origin as well as of the "virus disorders" may perhaps have been caused by GE [genetically engineered] foods.

As the Bt-toxin demonstratedly affects mouse intestines, it cannot be excluded that it might cause disturbances in humans as well, manifesting as "foodborne disease with unknown origin". Biotech proponents assert that this toxin is degraded by stomach acid (although it is actually quite acid resistant). People may have a low level of gastric acid because of disease or because of the very common use of Losec or similar potent antacid preparations. In addition, there may exist a genetic variability in the susceptibility to the toxic effect, so that a minority of the population is especially sensitive. As the foods are not labelled as GE, the connection is not apparent to the consumer. According to Cummins, no studies have been done that reliably exclude this possibility.

2. Professor Joe Cummins has pointed out that certain bacterial DNA sequences present in practically all GE crops may increase the risk for inflammatory disorders. These so called CpG sequences are found in the DNA used for enabling gene insertion (vectors) and in many of the primary crop protection genes including Bt and most herbicide tolerance genes. This bacterial DNA contains considerable amounts of the CpG sequence (higher forms of life, so called eukaryocytes, have little of this sequence and it is in a different state). This sequence induces inflammation and may adversely affect autoimmune diseases like rheumatoid arthritis. It also acts as a promoter of lymphoma, a malignant blood disease.

Inflammation induced in the bowel by this bacterial DNA in GE foods might perhaps mimic foodborne diarrhea. As Cummins points out, it might also induce or worsen other inflammatory conditions.

There are two conceivable ways in which GE foods may cause gastrointestinal disturbances in addition to those proposed by Ho. It is through the presence of the common Bt toxin and through the very common presence of the CpG DNA sequence that induces inflammation. The large increase of assumed "virus foodborne" diseases and the large proportion of diseases with unknown cause justify a consideration of these alternatives.

9

Genetically Modified Foods Do Not Cause Food-Borne Illnesses

AgBiotechNet

AgBiotechNet is an online news service that publishes information about agricultural biotechnology for researchers, policy makers, and the agriculture industry worldwide.

There is no credible evidence that food from genetically modified (GM) plants causes food-borne illnesses in humans. The claim that individuals who eat GM foods will suffer allergic reactions is unsubstantiated, as is the assertion that GM foods lack nutritional value. Further, the risk of GM foods transmitting harmful viruses to people—which can cause food-borne illnesses—is negligible. Thus, consumers' fears about the safety of GM foods are unfounded.

C laims that foodstuffs containing ingredients from genetically modified [GM] plants are inherently less safe than their non-GM conventional counterparts remain unproven, according to a UK [United Kingdom] Royal Society policy statement.

In two submissions to the UK government-sponsored GM Science Review, the Royal Society argues that the potential for GM ingredients to reduce the nutritional quality of foods or to cause allergic reactions is in principle no different to that for non-GM ingredients. It says there is no credible evidence that human health can be damaged by eating DNA sequences created by the genetic modification of foodstuff ingredients. The statement suggests that any risks through allergenicity or inadvertant change in nutritional status would be equivalent to those encountered through traditional breeding. It also argues that health risks associated with specific viral DNA sequences[1] in GM plants are "negligible" and that DNA consumption from a wide variety of sources "poses no significant risk

---

1. Some consumers are concerned that specific viral DNA sequences in GM plants will combine with human DNA and produce new viruses that could cause foodborne illnesses.

to human health, and that additional ingestion of GM DNA has no effect".

Patrick Bateson, Vice-President and Biological Secretary of the Royal Society, said: "We conducted a major review of the evidence about GM plants and human health [2002], and we have not seen any evidence since then that changes our original conclusions. If credible evidence does exist that GM foods are more harmful to people than non-GM foods, we should like to know why it has not been made public."

No evidence of health risks

He added: "The public have been told for several years that GM foods are inherently unsafe to eat. Most people would like to know what evidence exists to back up such claims. We have examined the results of published research, and have found nothing to indicate that GM foods are inherently unsafe. If anybody does have convincing evidence, get it out in the open so that it can be evaluated."

"The public have a right to decide whether they want to buy GM foods, and are entitled to have access to sensible and informed advice, based on sound science. It is disappointing to find a group like Greenpeace stating on its website that 'the risks are enormous and the consequences potentially catastrophic,' without offering any solid reasons to support such a claim."

DNA consumption . . . "poses no significant risk to human health, and . . . additional ingestion of GM DNA has no effect."

Bateson continued: "Undoubtedly some important questions need to be answered about the potential impact, good or bad, of GM crops on the environment. But these should be addressed without a smokescreen of unfounded claims about their threat to human health."

He noted that a recent opinion poll showed that the majority of the UK public is opposed to GM foods. "Many consumers have been made anxious by unsubstantiated claims about the safety of GM foods," he said. "The developers of GM products also have not successfully demonstrated to consumers what benefits they offer compared to conventional foods."

The Society's submissions also draw attention to some areas of food regulation that it believes should be addressed to ensure that all foods, including those containing GM ingredients, are assessed properly. Bateson said: "The public expect regulations to keep abreast of new developments in the way food is made, and to be just as effective for both GM and non-GM foods. We understand that the Food Standards Agency has taken on board the recommendations we made in our report [in 2002] and is taking action to address the issues we highlighted."

10
Irradiation Helps Improve Food Safety

Randall Lutter

Randall Lutter is a fellow with the American Enterprise Institute (AEI)–Brookings Joint Center for Regulatory Studies. The American Enterprise Institute and the Brookings Institution established the AEI–Brookings Joint Center for Regulatory Studies to provide analyses of existing regulatory programs and new regulatory proposals.

Food irradiation can help reduce food-borne illnesses. All major international public health organizations have endorsed food irradiation as a risk-free, practical method for improving food safety, yet the U.S. Department of Agriculture and the Food and Drug Administration have been slow to approve the process. Criticism of food irradiation by several public interest groups and reluctance by grocers to offer irradiated foods are also barriers to making irradiated foods available in the United States. Despite those barriers, test marketing has shown that irradiation is well accepted by consumers.

Food-borne pathogens cause thousands of deaths and tens of millions of cases of food-borne illness each year in the United States. Although most food-borne illness involves only nausea and diarrhea, many people develop serious complications, including rheumatoid, cardiac, hepatic, and neurological problems. Food-borne disease is declining little if at all, despite major new food safety initiatives. The best way to prevent a substantial part of those deaths and illnesses is food irradiation, which all major international public health organizations have endorsed because it is safe and effective.

Irradiation is extremely effective at reducing pathogens. Irradiation of frozen ground meat products with a 7-kilogray (kGy) dose—a dose already approved by the U.S. Food and Drug Administration (FDA)—could eliminate *Escherichia coli* 0157:H7, a particularly hazardous pathogen. Irradiation destroys *Staphylococcus aureus* and *Campylobacter jejuni*, which are together responsible for more than 2.6 million food-borne illnesses per year, as effectively as it reduces *E. coli* 0157:H7. Reductions in numbers of viable organisms would be dramatic for other important pathogens: irradiation of meat reduces *Salmonella* levels by factors of 10 billion to 100 trillion. It is also effective for seafood, eggs, precooked meats, and produce.

Irradiation of food does not pose risks to consumers. The World Health Organization (WHO) has advised that "as long as sensory qualities of food are retained and harmful microorganisms destroyed, the actual amount of ionizing radiation applied is of secondary consideration." At high doses, irradiation can cause some loss of vitamins, but at currently permitted doses "—there's less vitamin degradation than you get with microwaving or cooking." Almost two decades ago, the WHO concluded that "irradiation of food up to an overall average dose of 10 kGy produced no toxicological hazard and introduced no special nutritional or microbiological problems." In 1997, WHO added that "food irradiation is perhaps the most thoroughly investigated food processing technology." It concluded that ". . . one can go as high as 75 kGy, as has already been done in some countries, and the result is the same—food is safe and wholesome and nutritionally adequate." Joining the WHO in endorsing food irradiation to improve food safety are the Codex Alimentarius Commission, the American Medical Association, the American Dietetic Association, and the health authorities of approximately 40 countries.

Market data in the United States suggest many informed consumers prefer irradiated foods. In retail trials, irradiated chicken had a market share of 43% when sold at the same price as other chicken. When sold for a 10% premium—a markup much greater than the costs of irradiation—its share of the market was about 25%. Indeed, many different types of medical, pharmaceutical, and consumer products are already irradiated.

Two government agencies are responsible

In the United States, two separate government agencies are responsible for regulation of food. The U.S. Department of Agriculture (USDA), through its Food Safety and Inspection Service, has responsibility for all meat and poultry and related products, whereas the Food and Drug Administration, part of the Department of Health and Human Services, regulates all other foods. According to the Federal Food, Drug, and Cosmetic Act, irradiation of food, including meat and poultry, is prohibited without a determination by the FDA that food irradiation at particular doses and for particular uses is safe. This dual, overlapping responsibility for irradiation of meat and poultry has contributed to delays in bringing irradiation of these foods to market.

Despite the well-established benefits of irradiation, federal regulations now permit irradiation to control pathogens only for poultry and spices. The USDA's regulations restrict poultry irradiation: it is permissible only at a dose of 3 kGy and with labeling statements that consumers can mistake for warnings. The USDA has proposed to allow meat irradiation and is expected to announce regulations this month.[1] Regulatory decisions to approve irradiation of seafood, precooked meats, and eggs, all of which are linked to food-borne illnesses and death, are years from com-

---

1. Meat irradiation regulations were approved in January 2001.

pletion. Faster government action could prevent illness and death associated with those foods.

Congress is partly responsible for delays in bringing food irradiation to market. The Federal Food, Drug, and Cosmetic Act defines sources of irradiation used to treat food as "food additives" and prohibits the use of food additives without an explicit determination of their safety. That definition delays the marketing of irradiated foods. In effect the Act directs FDA to address the wrong question—whether irradiation is safe—rather than whether food irradiation reduces risks to public health, taking into account both the reduced incidence of food-borne illness and any loss of safety from increased irradiation.

The regulatory agencies have also delayed the benefits of food irradiation by creating a redundant and complicated two-step approval process that is avoidable under current law. The first step is a determination by the FDA that food irradiation at particular doses is safe for particular uses. The second step is a determination by the USDA that the use of irradiation is in compliance with applicable FDA requirements, does not render the product adulterated or misbranded or otherwise out of compliance with the requirements of the Federal Meat Inspection Act, is functional and suitable for the product, and is permitted only at the lowest level necessary to accomplish the stated technical effect as determined in specific cases. The second step is required not by the Federal Food, Drug, and Cosmetic Act, but by USDA's interpretation of its own regulations, which prohibit use of a "substance" in the preparation of any meat product unless such a determination is made.

That two-step process, while arguably sensible for additives that do not improve public health, substantially delays delivery of the benefits of food irradiation to consumers. The FDA approved irradiation of meat 3 years after receiving a petition; however, the USDA, which must also approve, has taken two more years to issue its own rule. In their recent rulemakings about meat irradiation, the agencies do not cite any recent scientific discoveries confirming the safety of irradiation. Instead, they cite safety evidence most of which is 20 years old.

Anti-irradiation groups slow approval process

The slow pace of government approval of irradiation has causes more complex than bureaucratic inertia and lack of interagency leadership. Cautionary or critical positions taken by several public interest groups play a role. Food and Water, a stridently anti-irradiation group, has paid for advertisements and organized telephone and letter campaigns against food irradiation. Consumers Union, the publisher of *Consumer Reports*, has been studiously neutral on the subject. Other influential groups, including Center for Science in the Public Interest, National Consumers League and Consumer Federation of America take a slightly more supportive stand, but still manage to impede improvements in public health by advocating conspicuous labeling and even increased testing of irradiated foods. Such views, because they are presented by "public interest" groups, can deter agencies that seek to regulate by consensus from implementing regulatory changes that would promote public health, unless there is strong political leadership.

Industry has also been slow to irradiate poultry, although the USDA allowed it in 1992. The market share of irradiated poultry is only about 1%. Why isn't irradiated poultry found in supermarkets today, given that market trials suggest it could sell at a profit? One possible reason is that grocers may be reluctant to stock "safer" poultry because it would raise questions about the safety of their other poultry products. In addition, their contracts with major poultry suppliers may include volume discounts that discourage the introduction of new products that hurt established brands. Those explanations are not fully satisfactory, but they suggest that factors limiting market share include market barriers, as well as restrictions on labeling and dose. More creative marketing may be needed to bring irradiated foods to U.S. consumers.

Irradiation of meat, when approved by USDA, may become more widespread than poultry irradiation, because people like rare hamburgers. Many restaurants have already stopped selling medium-rare hamburgers because of safety concerns.

USDA must speed up approval

Although the USDA has recently proposed to allow irradiation of meat, the USDA's rulemaking is late and should have been expedited. Millions of illnesses and thousand of deaths per year could be avoided by irradiation of meats, and the USDA's delays postpone these benefits.

Furthermore, the USDA proposal is too limited. It would unnecessarily restrict producers' ability to market irradiated meats by mandating the content and placement of certain statements on food labels and by offering no guidelines for labeling claims like *"Salmonella*-free." It takes no steps to promote irradiation of precooked meats, eggs, and seafood. It would leave in place redundant testing requirements and performance standards for *Salmonella*.

There are several ways the government can improve its regulation of food irradiation. First, the USDA should not require any labeling that could be misinterpreted as a warning; instead, it should require only that irradiation be identified as food preservatives are now. In addition, the USDA should allow labels that inform consumers how irradiated foods reduce the risk of food-borne disease and death. Second, the USDA should revise its rules so that firms that irradiate at a given dose would be exempt from redundant requirements to test for pathogens on those products. Third, the FDA—which under the Act must determine the safety of irradiation at particular doses for particular purposes—should allow irradiation of precooked meats, eggs, and seafood.

Regulatory agencies will have to become much more supportive of food irradiation if consumers are to enjoy all the health benefits that it promises. The FDA should promptly determine that irradiation of any food is generally recognized as safe, based on the findings of the World Health Organization and other scientific and public health organizations. In addition, the White House should make up for its recent lack of leadership on this issue and demonstrate the benefits of irradiated food by serving irradiated turkey at the next state dinner.

11

Food Irradiation Is Dangerous and Ineffective

John M. LaForge

John M. LaForge is codirector of Nukewatch, an antiwar group, and editor of its quarterly newsletter, the Pathfinder. *His articles have appeared in* Z Magazine, Earth Island Journal, *and the* Progressive.

Irradiation of food has not been proven to be a safe, effective method of reducing food-borne illnesses. It does not kill all disease-causing pathogens, especially viruses, and no studies of long-term effects of eating irradiated foods have been conducted. Further, irradiation destroys B vitamins and changes the taste and aroma of meat. Because food irradiation uses cesium-137, a hazardous radioactive waste material, it endangers the workers who handle it and presents a potential risk of environmental contamination. For all these reasons, the government should prohibit irradiation of food until the safety of the process and the wholesomeness of irradiated food can be guaranteed.

The same folks that brought you open-air bomb testing, human radiation experiments, Three Mile Island,[1] and Chernobyl[2] are promoting the food irradiation process. Ever since 1986, the FDA [Food and Drug Administration], the nuclear industry, and the meat industry have moved to expose almost the entire food supply to nuclear irradiation. But staunch citizen opposition has generally kept the business out of use. For 14 years, Food & Water,[3] and thousands of individuals have kept poultry, fruits, and vegetables free of irradiation. But the struggle is on to keep the meat supply out of this risky business.

According to an August 1997 "CBS News" poll, 73 percent are against irradiation and 77 percent say they wouldn't eat irradiated food.

1. The accident at the Three Mile Island nuclear power plant near Middletown, Pennsylvania, on March 28, 1979, was the most serious in U.S. nuclear power plant history.   2. The accident at the Chernobyl nuclear power plant in the Ukranian republic of the former Soviet Union on April 26, 1986, was the worst in the history of nuclear power. Over two hundred thousand people were evacuated from the area.   3. Food & Water is a national nonprofit organization that educates the general public about various threats to the food and water supply.

John M. LaForge, "Food Irradiation and Nuclear Weapons," *Z Magazine*, vol. 13, October 2000, pp. 36–39. Copyright © 2000 by John M. LaForge. Reproduced by permission.

How irradiation works

Food is irradiated using radioactive gamma ray sources, usually radioactive cobalt-60 or cesium-137, or high-energy electron beams. After packaging and being put into large metal boxes, the foods are placed on conveyor belts that move past the radiation sources. The materials are hit with the equivalent of 30 million X-rays, (according to the Spring 1998 *Food & Water* journal). The industry now uses cobalt-60 supplied by the Canadian company Nordion International, Inc. But the only isotope available in sufficient quantities for large-scale irradiation is cesium-137. When not in use the cobalt or cesium is lowered into cooling ponds.

In the process, which takes about 20 to 30 minutes, the gamma radiation passes through the food, killing all bacteria (helpful as well as harmful) and slowing decay but not leaving the food radioactive.

Irradiated food "will cost more, contain slightly reduced levels of B vitamins, endanger workers, and risk environmental contamination."

Irradiators are used on the meats at the end of the production line, after it is already sealed in packages. This is particularly important in ground beef, where bacteria can easily get beneath the surface during grinding. However the industry is lobbying for approval of irradiating unpackaged meats as well.

Cesium-137 is radioactive waste left in huge quantities from nuclear weapons production at Hanford in Washington State and Savannah River, South Carolina. A by-product of nuclear reactor operation, cesium-137 is an extremely hazardous isotope that is deadly for 600 years. It is water-soluble, which makes it terribly dangerous in the event of an accident. As radioactive waste, it is extremely expensive to store and keep out of the biosphere.

The Department of Energy admitted to the House Armed Services Committee in 1983: "The utilization of these radioactive materials simply reduces our waste handling problem. . .we get some of these very hot elements like cesium and strontium out of the waste" (Michael Colby, ed., "Food Irradiation: Why it Must Be Stopped and How We Can Do It, An Activist Primer," *Food & Water*, 1998). Dr. Rosalie Bertell (a renowned epidemiologist from Toronto [Canada]) explains that irradiation is a convenient excuse to reprocess spent irradiated fuel rods from weapons production reactors.

FDA spokesperson Jim Greene said in 1986 that using the cesium-137 "could substantially reduce the cost of disposing of nuclear waste" (*Grand Forks Herald*, 28 April 1986).

Irradiation changes nutrient content

The gamma rays break up the molecular structure of food, forming positively and negatively charged particles called "free radicals." The free radicals react with the food to create new chemical substances called "radiolytic products." The radiolytic products unique to the irradiation process are called "unique radiolytic products" (URPs). Some radiolytic products, such as formaldehyde, benzene, formic acid, and quinones are harmful to human health. Benzene is a known carcinogen. Some URPs are completely new chemicals that have not been identified, let alone tested for toxicity. URPs were somehow given a blanket exemption by the FDA from the safety testing required of other food additives.

Although the FDA says irradiation doesn't change nutritional content, the process does destroy nutrients essential to human health, such as vitamins C, E, K, and B-complex. (Vitamin E levels can be reduced by 25 percent after irradiation and vitamin C by 5–10 percent. Irradiation is ineffective against viruses.)

Radiation doses at the levels recommended will not kill all microorganisms. Typically, 90 percent may be destroyed and this means that the food still has to be treated with care otherwise the remaining organisms will reproduce rapidly. While the government and meat industry claim the flavor and aroma of the treated meats doesn't change, taste testers have disagreed.

Food Editor for the *New York Times*, Marian Burrows, writes, "Well-cooked conventional meat still tastes better. A blind tasting of irradiated and conventional ground beef, as well as steaks, pork loin and chicken makes it clear that the meat industry has its work cut out for it . . . all the irradiated meat smelled funny, especially the ground beef . . . barnyard odor . . . like steamed cow" (*New York Times*, December 10, 1997).

There has been no study of the effects of a long-term diet of irradiated foods.

Foods already approved for irradiation include beef, pork, poultry, nuts, potatoes, wheat, wheat flour, fruits, and vegetables, as well as all teas, and 60 dried herbs and spices. The nuclear industry also irradiates medical equipment, food containers, cosmetics, tampons, adhesive bandages, and cleaning solutions for contact lenses. A short chronology of the approval process looks like this:

- In 1953, food irradiation was named part of the so-called "atoms for peace" programs and the Army began research. In 1958 irradiation was classified as a food additive, requiring safety testing.
- In 1963, the FDA approved irradiation for bacon, but later banned it, having learned of "deficiencies" in the Army's research data on which the FDA had based its approval (*Ms Magazine*, November 1985).
- The FDA, in 1968, re-approved the use of irradiation for bacon, for killing insects in wheat and wheat flour, and for the inhibition of sprouting in potatoes.
- In 1983, the FDA approved sterilization of spices with irradiation. Low-dose irradiation can also be used to inhibit sprouting of onions, garlic, and ginger, and to inhibit the ripening of bananas, avocados, mangoes, papayas, and guavas. Hawaii is being pushed hard to open large irradiators for treating these tropical fruits.

- In 1996, the FDA gave permission for the expanded use of irradiation in the U.S. food supply.
- 1997 saw FDA approval of irradiation for beef and other red meats such as lamb (MLWK *Journal* and St. Paul *Pioneer*, December 3, 1997).

Hide the label, they will buy

In 1999, the U.S. Department of Agriculture (USDA) proposed rules and regulations for labeling the food and for licensing the factories that may do the irradiating. The rule-making process brought to light a horrifying series of accidents and contamination.

The meat industry lobbied vigorously for the 1997 bill on irradiation as an alternative to Clinton administration proposals for greater government authority to recall contaminated meat and punish violators. This is why professional critics of the process are so alarmed.

Former Assistant Secretary of Agriculture Carol Tucker Forman writes that irradiation sterilizes dirty meat, "but it doesn't keep meat from being recontaminated. Every time the meat is handled, from packing plant to grocery store to a home stove, it can come into contact with disease-causing bacteria. The meat might pass through a contaminated grinder, or it could be mixed with scraps that have been sitting in the store for a while" (*New York Times*, December 5, 1997).

Michael Jacobson, executive director of the Center for Science in the Public Interest opposes irradiation and writes that irradiated food "will cost more, contain slightly reduced levels of B vitamins, endanger workers, and risk environmental contamination" (letters, *NYT*, December 8, 1997).

The 1997 bill also changed labeling requirements for all foods treated with irradiation, so that the words: "Treated with Irradiation," need be no larger than those of the ingredient list.

However, the FDA requires no labeling of irradiated ingredients, so potato soup made with irradiated potatoes, onions, and spices need not be so labeled. Today, the industry is lobbying hard to eliminate all labeling requirements for irradiated foods.

An illustrative parallel is found in the use of GMOs (genetically modified organisms). In Europe, foods containing GMOs require labeling. This may explain why Europeans are more educated on the subject and why the European Union banned the import of U.S. GMOs. However, in the U.S. where no labeling of GMOs is required nearly 65 percent of foods on supermarket shelves contain ingredients that are genetically modified.

FDA approval is no guarantee of safety

FDA troubles with prescription drugs don't inspire confidence in its "okay" for irradiation. After 80 deaths were attributed to the heartburn medicine Propulsid, the FDA is considering a severe restriction and the manufacturer has withdrawn it. The action came on the heels of the Rzulin scare. FDA ordered it off the market after it was linked to 63 deaths.

There has been no study of the effects of a long-term diet of irradiated foods. The FDA reviewed 441 toxicity studies to determine the safety of irradiated foods. The team leader in charge of the review testified that all 441 studies were flawed. The FDA now claims that only 6 of the 441 were "properly conducted, fully adequate by 1980 standards, and able to stand alone in support of safety."

One of these six showed a statistically significant increase in stillbirth rates among rats fed irradiated wheat. Another reported unexplained deaths and abnormalities in animals given irradiated food, not reaching statistical significance because of the small number of animals in the study. Both studies used irradiation levels well below the proposed levels for human food. Dr. Bertell concludes: "Thus the 'scientific' evidence in support of food irradiation consists of studies with low irradiation dose, small number of animals, short follow-up times, and negative results. No real scientist would accept these studies as establishing the safety of irradiated foods."

With this shabby hobbled-together assurance of just five studies, the FDA approved irradiation for the public food supply.

Food caterers, restaurants, retirement homes, childcare centers, hospitals and schools are not required to inform clients that their foods are irradiated (Minneapolis *Star Tribune*, December 16, 1999).

Without a guarantee of start-to-finish safety, from the handling of radioactive source materials to the long-term consumption of irradiated foods, irradiation should be prohibited.

The facilities that irradiate foods and equipment have caused accidents that must not be repeated. The NRC [National Response Center] has recorded 54 accidents at 132 irradiation facilities worldwide since 1974. Unhappily, expanding irradiation will increase the number of radiation accidents by increasing the handling and high-speed transportation of radioactive "source" materials on railroads and highways. It will expose factory surroundings and industry workers to radioactive spills and leaks. Indeed irradiation's "Three Mile Island" has already happened.

In Decatur, Georgia, Radiation Sterilizers, Inc. (RSI) got 252 21-inch canisters of cesium-137 (which were never designed for use at an irradiation facility) from the Department of Energy. In 1988 RSI began using the cesium-137 to irradiate spices. After only two years, a cesium-137 capsule began leaking into the storage pool. It took federal officials six months to find the leak's source. Contaminated workers took the poison home with them. In 1992, the contaminated building was abandoned, and RSI took the word "radiation" out of its name. Now they're "Sterigenics" (*Food & Water Journal*, Spring 1998).

Neither the FDA nor the nuclear industry has demonstrated an ability to safeguard the public from its deadly man-made radiation. Without a guarantee of start-to-finish safety, from the handling of radioactive source materials to the long-term consumption of irradiated foods, irradiation should be prohibited.

The priorities for governments and their food inspectors should be: (1) improving food harvesting, storage and manufacturing processes; and (2) eliminating or containing the contamination that has found its way into the food chain.

12

Federal Inspection Makes America's Meat Safe

Kerri B. Harris

Kerri B. Harris is executive director of the International HACCP Alliance at Texas A&M University. The International HACCP (Hazard Analysis and Critical Control Point) Alliance helps provide a uniform program to assure safe meat and poultry.

Federal meat inspection laws initiated in the last century and continually updated make the meat industry the most highly regulated food industry in the country. Daily inspections of processing plants and packing establishments by U.S. Department of Agriculture (USDA) and Food Safety and Inspection Service (FSIS) employees ensure the safety of American meat. The Hazard Analysis and Critical Control Point (HACCP) rule, which became part of the federal inspection laws on July 25, 1996, requires the reduction of *Salmonella* and *E. coli* pathogens in meat and the development and implementation of a system to identify food safety hazards. The use of Sanitation Standard Operating Procedures (SSOPs) to prevent direct meat contamination or adulteration was also part of the HACCP rule. Further, FSIS has an ongoing chemical monitoring program to detect and prevent the misuse of chemicals such as antibiotics in livestock production.

The safety of meat products and the protection of public health are primary concerns for the beef industry. Throughout the past few years and even today, there are many food safety challenges facing the industry. The industry has completed and is currently conducting research, identifying new and improved technologies, and exploring all opportunities to strengthen the safety of today's meat supply. The beef industry is dedicated to producing the highest quality and safest beef products for consumers.

Government oversight is not new to the meat industry, but it has continued to change. In 1906, the meat industry was heavily criticized in *The Jungle* written by Upton Sinclair for poor working environments and

Kerri B. Harris, "Meat Inspection Overview," *Beef Facts*, 2002. Copyright © 2002 by Cattlemen's Beef Board and the National Cattlemen's Beef Association, www.beef.org. Reproduced by permission.

producing meat under insanitary conditions. Congress responded to the public demands for improved working conditions and better sanitation by passing the Federal Meat Inspection Act (FMIA) of 1906, which was amended in 1967 by the Wholesome Meat Act. In late 1992 and early 1993, there was an outbreak of *Escherichia coli* O157:H7 which caused some people to question the safety of meat products, especially ground beef. Partly in response to the public concern, the United States Department of Agriculture's (USDA) Food Safety and Inspection Service (FSIS) released the 1996 Pathogen Reduction/Hazard Analysis and Critical Control Point (PR/HACCP) final rule, which mandated the implementation of HACCP throughout the meat industry.

Meat inspection

Under the Meat Act the USDA/FSIS inspects all meat sold in interstate commerce and re-inspects imported products to ensure they fulfill all U.S. requirements. As of August 2002, the FSIS had over 9,000 full-time employees serving to ensure that all regulatory requirements are met in approximately 6,200 federally inspected establishments. Unlike the Food and Drug Administration's (FDA) inspection system that has periodic visits by inspectors to food establishments, FSIS inspectors are in the establishments each and every day to ensure that the products are fit for human consumption and in compliance with all Federal laws governing the wholesomeness and safety of meat products. Therefore, the meat industry is truly the most highly regulated food industry in the country.

To provide this extensive oversight, FSIS maintains a comprehensive system of controls, some of which are outlined below.

Humane handling and antemortem inspections

The inspection process starts with the live animal. Antemortem inspection involves a visual and physical evaluation of the live animal prior to slaughter to identify any conditions that may indicate disease or illness. The inspection personnel are responsible for identifying any high-risk animals and making determinations to allow them to enter the food chain or to condemn them from entering. These actions are taken to ensure that meat is safe and wholesome for consumption.

Humane handling has long been of interest to both the Agency and the industry. The beef industry has studied the behavior and movement of cattle and designed pens, walkways and equipment to improve the handling of livestock. In early 2002 the FSIS placed 17 District Veterinary Medical Specialists (DVMS) in the field to deal specifically with the oversight of humane handling issues. Strict guidelines are in place and strongly enforced to prevent the mishandling of animals.

Postmortem inspections

The inspectors are responsible for conducting a thorough examination of the lymph nodes, organs, and entire carcass to identify signs of disease and unwholesome conditions. This inspection process involves all slaughtered animals. The postmortem inspection allows inspectors to further evaluate the carcass and tissues from any animal they suspected to be a high risk during antemortem inspection before a final decision on product use is determined. If any carcass or its parts are identified as diseased or unwholesome then they are condemned and prevented from entering the food supply. This is a complete system to prevent diseased animals from entering the food supply.

Product inspections

The inspection system continues throughout the entire processing segment of the industry, including both raw and fully cooked products. Processing inspectors are responsible for processed meat products and all other ingredients contained in the finished product. These inspectors are responsible for cured and smoked products, frozen dinners, canned meats, and other processed products. They must verify that the establishment is maintaining sanitary conditions and following all procedures and labeling regulations.

Hazard Analysis and Critical Control Point (HACCP) rule

The use of HACCP as a process control for food safety is not new to the food industry or to the meat industry. Many establishments were utilizing HACCP before the release of FSIS' Pathogen Reduction/HACCP final rule on July 25, 1996. However, the release of the HACCP rule is probably the most significant change for meat inspection since the 1967 amendment to the Act.

As the name implies, there are two components to the 1996 rule—1) the reduction of pathogens, and 2) the development and implementation of HACCP systems. The pathogen reduction part of the rule includes the *Salmonella* Performance Standard and the generic *E. coli* testing. The regulation was phased in over a three-year period with the final implementation dates in early 2000. Today, all federally and state inspected establishments are operating under a HACCP system and all new establishments must have a HACCP Inspected Meat system developed before receiving a grant of inspection.

Under the Meat Act the USDA/FSIS inspects all meat sold in interstate commerce and re-inspects imported products to ensure they fulfill all U.S. requirements.

HACCP allows establishments to identify food safety hazards that are reasonably likely to occur in the process or type of product being produced and establish points of control to prevent them from occurring. HACCP is a science-based process control system that focuses on preventing food safety problems. The role of the FSIS inspector in a HACCP system is to verify that the establishment has developed and is implementing the HACCP system as designed. In late 2001, the FSIS introduced the Consumer Safety Officer (CSO) positions that report to the district offices. The CSO is responsible for conducting a comprehensive assessment of the establishment's food safety system to see if it is an adequately designed and supportable program that will control food safety hazards.

Residue and microbiological testing

FSIS has an on-going residue monitoring program to detect and prevent the misuse of chemicals (i.e., antibiotics) during the production of livestock. The Agency is responsible for identifying any high-risk animals and collecting samples for laboratory analysis to determine if violative levels of chemical residues are present. The industry has been working with the Agency to continue to decrease the possibility of chemical contamination by promoting educational programs for livestock producers and implementing quality systems, such as the Beef Quality Assurance (BQA) program. Through the efforts of both the Agency and the industry, the risk of chemical residues in beef will continue to decline.

The meat industry is truly the most highly regulated food industry in the country.

Microbiological contamination is another major issue facing the meat industry. Pathogens such as *Listeria monocytogenes* and *Salmonella* are concerns on fully cooked, ready-to-eat products. The industry has conducted extensive research to learn more about environmental contamination in operations producing ready-to-eat foods to help minimize the risk of *Listeria monocytogenes* and other pathogens on fully cooked products. The FSIS personnel randomly select finished products to test for these pathogens. Any products that are found to be contaminated will be prevented from entering the food supply or will be recalled if already in commerce.

In 1994, FSIS declared that raw ground beef contaminated with the pathogen *E. coli* O157:H7 is adulterated and must be further processed to kill the microorganism or destroyed. This was the first time the presence of bacteria in a raw meat product was defined as an adulterant. FSIS also initiated a microbiological testing program to detect *Escherichia coli* O157:H7 in raw ground beef. As of Oct. 7, 2002, 42 out of more than 5,000 samples collected have tested positive for *E. coli* O157:H7. Inspected establishments and retail outlets are randomly selected for sample collection. Imported ground beef products are also subjected to sample collection by FSIS Import Inspection personnel and ground beef products produced at state inspected establishments are collected by state program personnel.

Sanitation

The HACCP final rule also required the development and implementation of Sanitation Standard Operating Procedures (SSOPs). These programs are intended to prevent direct product contamination or adulteration, and focus on pre-operational and operational activities. Every establishment must develop, implement, and maintain effective SSOPs. Also, the Sanitation Requirements for Official Meat and Poultry Establishments Final Rule became effective on January 25, 2000. This rule established performance standards for sanitation and was designed to consolidate the sanitation regulations into a single rule applicable to both meat and poultry. Section 416.1 of the rule states, "Each official establishment must be operated and maintained in a manner to prevent the creation of insanitary conditions and to ensure that product is not adulterated."

The USDA inspection legend

The USDA's Food Safety and Inspection Service has authority over the production of wholesome and safe meat products. Each federally inspected establishment is granted an establishment number that is placed on the official inspection legend. The inspection legend is stamped onto carcasses at various locations and placed onto product labels of packaged meats. The application of the inspection legend means that the operation has complied with all of the Agency's regulatory requirements.

Meat production is the most highly regulated food industry. The USDA's Food Safety and Inspection Service is responsible for developing rules and regulations for the production of wholesome and safe foods and providing regulatory oversight during the day-to-day production. However, the beef industry understands and accepts its responsibility in producing the safest product possible. The combination of regulatory oversight and the commitment and dedication of the industry should allow consumers to purchase and prepare meat products with confidence in the safety of the product. Food safety begins with the establishment, includes regulatory verification, and ends with the consumer. Working together— the USDA's Food Safety and Inspection Service, the beef industry, and the consumer—we can make a winning team for the safest beef supply in the world.

13

Federal Inspection Does Not Adequately Ensure Meat Safety

Eric Schlosser

Eric Schlosser is an investigative journalist and author of Fast Food Nation: The Dark Side of the All-American Meal, *an exposé of fast-food chains.*

America's federal meat inspection laws are not strict enough to protect consumers from food-borne pathogens such as *E.coli* and *Salmonella*. Further, the U.S. Department of Agriculture (USDA) lacks the ability to enforce those laws. Specifically, the USDA has no power to force a meat packer to recall meat even when high levels of pathogens are found in the company's products; recall of tainted meat is strictly voluntary. Often, as in the case of the ConAgra recall in July 2002, meat packers only take action after people become ill. The USDA cannot effectively carry out its dual and conflicting mandate—to promote the sale of American meat and at the same time protect consumers from unsafe meat. Only the creation of an independent food safety agency with aggressive enforcement powers will protect consumers from food-borne illnesses caused by unsafe meat.

In a summer full of headlines about corporate misdeeds and irresponsibility, ConAgra's massive recall in July [2002] stands apart. The defective product wasn't fiber optic cable, energy futures or some esoteric financial instrument. It was bad meat—almost 19 million pounds of beef potentially contaminated with *E. coli* O157:H7, enough to supply a tainted burger to at least one-fourth of the US population. Unlike other prominent scandals, this one does not seem to involve any falsification of records, shredding of crucial documents or deliberate violation of the law. And that makes it all the more disturbing. The Bush Administration and its Republican allies in Congress have allowed the meatpacking industry to gain control of the nation's food safety system, much as the airline industry was given responsibility for airport security in the years leading up to the September 11, [2001] attacks. The deregulation of food safety makes about as much sense as the deregulation of air safety. Anyone who eats meat these days should be deeply concerned about what our meatpacking companies now have the freedom to sell.

Anyone who eats meat these days should be deeply concerned about what our meatpacking companies now have the freedom to sell.

At the heart of the food safety debate is the issue of microbial testing. Consumer advocates argue that the federal government should be testing meat for dangerous pathogens and imposing tough penalties on companies that repeatedly fail those tests. The meatpacking industry, which has been battling new food safety measures for almost a century, strongly disagrees. In 1985 a panel appointed by the National Academy of Sciences warned that the nation's meat inspection system was obsolete. At the time USDA inspectors relied solely on visual and olfactory clues to detect tainted meat. After the Jack in the Box outbreak in 1993, the Clinton Administration announced that it would begin random testing for *E. coli* O157:H7 in ground beef. The meatpacking industry promptly sued the USDA in federal court to block such tests.

E. coli O157:H7, the pathogen involved in both the Jack in the Box outbreak and the recent ConAgra recall, can cause severe illness or death, especially among children, the elderly and people who are immunosuppressed. The Centers for Disease Control and Prevention (CDC) estimate that about 73,000 Americans are sickened by *E. coli* O157:H7 every year. An additional 37,000 are sickened by other dangerous strains of *E. coli* also linked to ground beef. At a slaughterhouse these pathogens are spread when manure or stomach contents get splattered on the meat.

Company employees conduct inspections

The USDA won the 1993 lawsuit, began random testing for *E. coli* O157:H7 and introduced a "science-based" inspection system in 1996 that requires various microbial tests by meatpacking companies and by the government. The new system, however, has been so weakened by industry opposition and legal challenges that it now may be less effective than the old one. Under the Hazard Analysis and Critical Control Points plans that now regulate production at meatpacking plants, many food safety tasks have been shifted from USDA inspectors to company employees.

In return for such concessions, the USDA gained the power to test for *salmonella* and to shut down plants that repeatedly failed those tests. *Salmonella* is spread primarily by fecal material, and its presence in ground beef suggests that other dangerous pathogens may be present as well. In November 1999, the USDA shut down a meatpacking plant for repeatedly failing *salmonella* tests. The Texas company operating the plant, Supreme Beef Processors, happened to be one of the leading suppliers of ground beef to the National School Lunch Program. With strong backing from the meatpacking industry, Supreme Beef sued the USDA, eventually won the lawsuit and succeeded this past December [2001] in overturning the USDA's *salmonella* limits. About 1.4 million Americans are sickened by *salmonella* every year, and the CDC has linked a nasty, antibiotic-resistant strain of the bug to ground beef. Nevertheless, it is now perfectly legal to sell ground beef that is thoroughly contaminated with *salmonella*—and sell it with the USDA's seal of approval.

This summer's ConAgra recall raises questions not only about the nation's food safety rules but also about the USDA's competence to enforce them. The USDA conducts its random tests for *E. coli* O157:H7 at wholesale and retail locations, not at the gigantic slaughterhouses where the meat is usually contaminated. By the time the USDA discovers tainted meat, it's already being distributed. On June 17 and 19, [2002] USDA test results showed that beef shipped from the ConAgra slaughterhouse in Greeley, Colorado was contaminated. But the USDA failed to inform ConAgra for almost two weeks. Meanwhile, the bad meat continued to be sold at supermarkets, served at countless restaurants and grilled at outdoor barbecues nationwide. Although the packages said "Freeze or sell by 06 18 02," Safeway supermarkets in Colorado held a two-for-one sale of the questionable ConAgra meat from June 19 to June 25.

ConAgra's recall was "voluntary"

Four days later the USDA informed ConAgra that it had distributed beef contaminated with *E. coli* O157:H7, ConAgra announced a "voluntary recall" of 354,200 pounds. Then health authorities noticed that people were getting severely ill, mainly small children in Colorado. A common symptom was vomiting and defecating blood. After consultations with the USDA, ConAgra expanded the voluntary recall on July 19 to include an additional 18.3 million pounds of beef processed at the Greeley plant between April 12 and July 11. About three dozen illnesses and one death have thus far [September 2002] been linked to ConAgra's meat. Based on previous *E. coli* outbreaks, perhaps twenty times that number of illnesses occurred without being properly diagnosed or reported. According to the most recent tally, less than one-tenth of the 18.6 million pounds of ConAgra's recalled meat has been recovered. The rest has most likely been eaten.

America's food safety system has been expertly designed not to protect the public health but to protect the meatpacking industry from liability.

Throughout the recall, USDA officials praised ConAgra for how well it had cooperated with the government, offering little criticism or explanation of how this company had managed to ship thousands of tons of potentially contaminated meat for months. The USDA also deflected criticism of its own role in the outbreak; a Montana wholesaler had warned the agency in February that beef shipped from ConAgra's plant in Greeley was tainted. Instead of imposing a tough penalty on ConAgra, the USDA often seemed eager to shift the blame and responsibility to consumers. "If people cooked their food correctly," said Elsa Murano, USDA under secretary for food safety, "a lot of outbreaks would not take place."

When most people learn how the meatpacking industry operates, they're appalled.

Although ConAgra apparently violated no laws, its behavior made clear where the real power lies. The recall of its meat was entirely voluntary. In an age when defective Happy Meal toys can be swiftly ordered off the market at the slightest hint of a choking hazard, the government can neither demand the recall of potentially deadly meat nor impose civil fines on companies that sell it. ConAgra has refused to disclose publicly which restaurants, distributors and supermarkets got meat from Greeley; federal law does not require the company to do so. Colorado health officials did not receive a list showing where ConAgra's meat had been distributed until the first week of August—more than a month after the initial recall. Health officials in Utah and Oklahoma did not receive that information from ConAgra until the third week in August. "I know it's here," an Oklahoma public health official told the *Denver Post* at one point, referring to the recalled meat. "But without knowing where it went, there's not a whole lot we can do." In future recalls, ConAgra now promises to do a better job of sharing information with state health authorities—even though the law does not require the company to do so.

Excessive line speeds cause problems

ConAgra's meatpacking operations in Greeley are described at length in my book *Fast Food Nation*, and I've spent a great deal of time with workers there. For years they have complained about excessive line speeds. The same factors often responsible for injuries in a slaughterhouse can also lead to food safety problems. When workers work too fast, they tend to make mistakes, harming themselves or inadvertently contaminating the meat.

America's food safety system has been expertly designed not to protect the public health but to protect the meatpacking industry from liability. The industry has received abundant help in this effort from the Republican Party, which for more than a decade has thwarted Congressional efforts to expand the USDA's food safety authority. According to the Center for Responsive Politics, during the 2000 presidential campaign meat and livestock interests gave about $23,000 to [Democrat] Al Gore and about $600,000 to [Republican] George W. Bush. The money was well spent. Dale Moore, chief of staff for Agriculture Secretary Ann Veneman, was previously the chief lobbyist for the National Cattlemen's Beef Association [NCBA]. Elizabeth Johnson, one of Veneman's senior advisers, was previously the associate director for food policy at the NCBA. Mary Waters, USDA assistant secretary for Congressional relations, assumed the post after working as legislative counsel for ConAgra Foods.

It would be an understatement to say that the Bush Administration has been friendly toward the big meatpackers. During Congressional testimony this past spring [2002], Elsa Murano, USDA chief food safety advocate, argued that her agency does not need the power to order a recall of contaminated meat. Nor did it need, she said, any new authority to shut down ground beef plants because of *salmonella* contamination.

New, tougher legislation

The meatpacking companies don't want any of their customers to get sick. But they don't want to be held liable for illnesses either, or to spend more money on preventing outbreaks. The exemplary food safety system at Jack in the Box increases the cost of the fast food chain's ground beef by about one penny per pound. The other major hamburger chains also require that their suppliers provide meat largely free of dangerous pathogens—and that requirement has not yet driven the meatpacking industry into bankruptcy. Senator Tom Harkin has introduced two pieces of food safety legislation that would help fill some of the glaring gaps in the current system.[1] The SAFER Meat, Poultry and Food Act of 2002 would give the USDA the authority to demand recalls of contaminated meat and impose civil fines on meatpacking companies. The Meat and Poultry Pathogen Reduction Act would place enforceable limits on the amounts of disease-causing bugs that meat can legally contain. Harkin's bills embody a good deal of common sense. Companies that produce clean meat should be allowed to sell it; those that produce dirty meat shouldn't. The Republican Party's alliance with the big meatpackers does not reflect widespread public support. The issue of food safety isn't like abortion or gun control, with passionate and fundamentally opposing views held by millions of American voters. When most people learn how the meatpacking industry operates, they're appalled. The outrage crosses party lines. Democrat or Republican, you still have to eat.

None of the recently proposed reforms, however, would prove as important and effective as the creation of an independent food safety agency with tough enforcement powers. The USDA has a dual and conflicting mandate. It's supposed to promote the sale of American meat—and protect consumers from unsafe meat. As long as the USDA has that dual role, consumers must be extremely careful about where they purchase beef, how they handle it and how long they cook it. While many Americans fret about the risks of bioterrorism, a much more immediate threat comes from the all-American meal. Until fundamental changes are made in our food safety system, enjoying your hamburgers medium-rare will remain a form of high-risk behavior.

1. As of August 2003, neither piece of legislation had passed.

14
Private Inspection Would Improve Meat Safety

E.C. Pasour Jr.

E.C. Pasour Jr. is an economist at North Carolina State University.

Private inspection firms driven by market incentives can provide consumers with more effective safeguards against tainted meat than federal inspection. A private firm inspecting meatpacking plants would be profitable only as long as its inspections accurately reflected the quality of the meat. If consumers became ill after eating meat inspected by a particular firm, that firm would soon go out of business. Thus, the profit incentive would stimulate more careful inspection of meat as well as the development of new methods to detect and destroy pathogens.

Last year's [1997] news reports of tainted beef focused public attention on the safety of the meat supply. In August 1997, Secretary of Agriculture Dan Glickman forced Hudson Foods to recall 25 million pounds of hamburger meat produced at the firm's state-of-the-art plant in Nebraska. The nation's largest beef recall occurred after several Colorado consumers became sick from hamburgers linked to *E. coli* contamination.

Examples of illness rooted in unsafe meat are not isolated incidents. Bad or undercooked meat causes an estimated 4,000 deaths and 5 million illnesses annually, according to the federal government's Centers for Disease Control. Moreover, a single incident of contaminated meat has the potential to affect large numbers of people. In 1993, five hundred people became ill and four children died in the Pacific northwest as a result of eating tainted hamburgers.

Illness and death caused by bad meat (whether tainted or undercooked) inevitably evoke calls for more government regulation. It is ironic that increased government intervention is viewed as an antidote to tainted meat, despite the federal government's long-standing responsibility for meat inspection in the United States. Indeed, the Hudson Foods incident occurred only a year after President [Bill] Clinton announced the most sweeping changes in the government's meat-inspection system.

E.C. Pasour Jr., "We Can Do Better than Government Inspection of Meat," *The Freeman: Ideas on Liberty*, vol. 48, May 1998, pp. 290–95. Copyright © 1998 by the Foundation for Economic Education, Inc. Reproduced by permission.

Moreover, a federal inspector was based at the Hudson Foods plant to check the plant's procedures daily.

Chronic problems related to meat inspection and meat safety warrant increased scrutiny of the most appropriate method of inspecting meat. During recent decades, successful deregulation initiatives occurred in a number of areas including banking and transportation. This shows that market forces may provide an improvement over government regulation of economic activity, even when regulations are long-standing and widely accepted.

Is meat inspection different?

Skeptics, including even many market proponents, might say that the conventional analysis doesn't hold for government regulations protecting health—where slip-ups can be fatal. Problems of "government failure," however, may be worse than any market imperfections that government regulation is instituted to remedy. Thus, government failure would have even graver implications for health issues.

Is it possible that the free market could substitute for, and even improve on, the current system of federal meat inspection? The following analysis demonstrates that the problems in government meat inspection are similar to those that plague all other government regulation of economic activity. There is no way for government regulators to obtain the information and realize the incentives of the decentralized market process, whatever the area of economic activity. Thus, market inspection of the U.S. meat industry, when contrasted with the current system of federal regulation, is likely to reduce the incidence of illness associated with the consumption of unsafe meat.

Federal meat inspection—how it began

The Meat Inspection Act of 1891 was a major landmark in federal regulation of meat and, indeed, of federal regulation of economic activity in the United States. A review of the political economy of that era is helpful in understanding the impetus for government regulation. Most government intervention then and now, at least ostensibly, is in response to "market failure"—economic outcomes that fall short of "perfect competition." (All markets fail, of course, when measured against this criterion.)

Moreover, the 1891 act was instituted under false pretenses. It was a solution to a largely nonexistent problem—contaminated meat. There is no reliable evidence that tainted meat was a major factor in the adoption of the legislation. In a political-economic analysis of the era, Gary Libecap concludes that "the record does not indicate that the incidence of diseased cattle or their consumption was very great, and there is no evidence of a major health issue at that time over beef consumption." Government meat inspection, once in place, however, like many other government regulations, was soon viewed as necessary to protect consumers.

There is a great deal of evidence that the political impetus for the 1891 legislation was the consequence of rapidly changing economic conditions. Market dominance by Chicago meat-packers—primarily Swift, Armour, Morris, and Hammond—quickly followed the introduction of refrigeration around 1880. Refrigeration allowed for centralized, large-scale, and lower-cost slaughterhouses because of production, distribution, and transportation advantages. The four large Chicago firms accounted for about 90 percent of the cattle slaughtered in Chicago within a decade after the introduction of refrigeration.

The Chicago packers fundamentally changed demand and supply conditions in the meatpacking industry. Small, local slaughterhouses throughout the country were rapidly displaced because they could not compete with the lower-cost Chicago packers. Local slaughter firms, in response, charged that Chicago packers used diseased cattle and that their dressed beef was unsafe. The disease issue, as bogus as it apparently was, threatened both domestic demand and export markets for U.S. meat. Cattle raisers, especially those in the midwest, backed federal meat inspection to promote demand.

Cattle producers were also concerned about falling prices. Prices fell because the supply of cattle grew rapidly. But producers attributed the fall to their declining market power versus the Chicago packers—a charge that seemed credible because of the packers' size and concentration. Ostensibly to deal with the largely spurious allegations of unsafe meat and collusion by the Chicago packers, cattlemen, and local packers called for federal meat inspection and antitrust legislation. Enactment of the Sherman Act in 1890 and the Meat Inspection Act of 1891 were thus closely tied legislatively.

The Jungle and the Meat Inspection Act of 1906

The famous Meat Inspection Act of 1906 also was heavily influenced by false charges. Ideas have consequences, and public policy can be influenced by a popular book, such as Upton Sinclair's *The Jungle*—regardless of its merits. The muckraking novel focused on greed and abuse among Chicago meat-packers and government inspectors. The characters in *The Jungle* tell of workers falling into tanks, being ground up with animal parts, and being made into "Durham's Pure Leaf Lard."

Sinclair wrote *The Jungle* to ignite a socialist movement on behalf of America's workers. He did not even pretend to have actually witnessed or verified the horrendous conditions he ascribed to Chicago packing houses. Instead, he relied heavily on both his own imagination and hearsay. Indeed, a congressional investigation at the time found little substance in Sinclair's allegations.

It is ironic that increased government intervention is viewed as an antidote to tainted meat, despite the federal government's long-standing responsibility for meat inspection in the United States.

Nevertheless, the sensational allegations dramatically reduced the demand for meat. U.S. exports fell by half. Major meat-packers saw new regulations as the way to restore confidence, and they strongly endorsed the Meat Inspection Act of 1906, which expanded the scope of federal inspection to include smaller competitors.

Economic conditions back then were much different from today's. However, there is a lesson to be learned from that early period concerning government and free-market approaches to meat inspection.

The early legislation, for the most part, was not a response by government to a legitimate public-health threat. Congress enacted the 1891 act in response to political pressure by local meat-packers and cattle growers who felt victimized by the rise in power of the Chicago packers and by lower cattle prices. This legislation along with the Sherman Act and the Interstate Commerce Act, all enacted within a four-year period, represented a significant break with what had previously been considered an appropriate role for the federal government.

The 1906 Meat Inspection Act, too, was largely a response to the meat industry's financial problems rather than to a health threat. The earlier spate of interventionist legislation, however, had provided a new mandate for government regulation of economic activity that facilitated the passage of the 1906 act. Thus, the case of federal meat inspection is yet another example of [Austrian economist and social philosopher] Ludwig von Mises's insight that government intervention almost inevitably leads to further intervention.

Pitfalls of government regulation

Thus government meat inspection, like most other economic regulation, was instituted mainly because of favor-seeking: the use of time and money to harness the power of government for private ends. Favor-seeking is a negative-sum activity. The nation's output of goods and services decreases as resources are used to restrict competition rather than to expand production and exchange. Favor-seeking is just one example of "government failure."

Government intervention often is counter-productive because of information and incentive problems. The crucial economic problem confronting society is how to use people's specialized knowledge to best satisfy consumers. As Nobel laureate F.A. Hayek emphasized, government officials cannot obtain the information that motivates individual choice because that information, much of which is never articulated, is strongly linked to a particular time and place. Consequently, officials must base decisions on something other than the "public interest," if that term means the interests of the people who comprise the public.

Moreover, even if the information could be known, it is unlikely to be used most effectively. Government officials lack appropriate incentives because power and responsibility are separated. Those who make and administer laws do not bear the consequences of their actions, at least not to the same extent as private individuals. As shown below, markets generally are superior to government regulation because they cope better with information and incentive problems.

Related to the incentive problem is another flaw in the current system of meat inspection: the adverse effect of government regulation on innovation. That flaw is found in all alternatives to the decentralized market process.

In the absence of the profit motive, individuals have less incentive to discover and implement new technology in the inspection and handling of meat. No one knows, of course, which new technology will ultimately prove beneficial in meat inspection or in any other area. However, in the marketplace, if an innovation proves to be profitable the person responsible for it will receive a large part of the reward. Things are quite different in a centralized system. Under government regulation, the government employee who discovers or adopts a potentially superior technology is likely to receive only a small amount of additional compensation. On the other hand, if the innovation doesn't pan out, he will lose much less than the entrepreneur in a profit-and-loss system.

Market inspection of the U.S. meat industry . . . contrasted with . . . federal regulation, is likely to reduce the incidence of illness associated with the consumption of unsafe meat.

This fundamental difference between markets and government is highly important to innovation in the meat industry. The heart of U.S. meat inspection continues to be the "poke and sniff" method that relies on the eyes and noses of some 7,400 Department of Agriculture [USDA] inspectors. In 1997 a small Massachusetts company, SatCon Technology Corporation, working with a North Dakota–based group of ranchers, found a way to use lasers to find illness-causing pathogens such as *E. coli* and *salmonella* by scanning animal carcasses in slaughterhouses. Such technological innovation has the potential to revolutionize meat inspection in the United States.

But it is more likely to be adopted in a free market than in a government-regulated market. Since it has the potential to dramatically reduce both the amount of labor currently used in meat inspection and the rationale for government regulation, it is inconsistent with two important goals of any bureaucracy: maintaining jobs and expanding its operation.

Market competition versus government regulation

The experience of government control of economic activity shows why government meat inspection is likely to be inferior to free markets. Private inspection firms, which must meet the market test, have a greater incentive to be effective than do government regulators. A private firm providing information to consumers about meat quality will reap profits when successful and incur losses when not. Thus, if a private meat-grading service were to become lax in satisfying consumers, meat firms no longer would be willing to pay for the service. Consequently, the private firm not only has an advantage in obtaining the necessary information; it also has a greater incentive to use it in the interest of the public weal.

Moreover, profit-seeking firms are likely to have a greater incentive than government regulators to adhere to quality standards. Government inspectors get to know the people operating the plants they regulate. Strict enforcement of standards might create hardship for those people. For example, if meat is considered to be of marginal quality but not to pose a significant health threat, regulators may be inclined to overlook such infractions. In short, when contrasted with market regulation, government regulators have a smaller incentive to enforce safety regulations.

Numerous studies have shown the benefits from privatization. It is quite likely that problems of food safety would be dealt with better through the decentralized market process, which provides a greater opportunity for both business firms and consumers to achieve their goals. Stated differently, the market process provides a greater incentive than government regulation for private firms and consumers to discover, disseminate, and use information about the quality of meat.

For one thing, government regulation gives consumers a false sense of security. It leads them to assume that they are being protected by the government, reducing the incentive to do their own checking. Market methods of inspection, in contrast, give consumers a greater incentive to acquire information about the quality of meat. Consequently, they are likely to be more alert to potential problems of food safety.

It is true, of course, that meat may be contaminated when it appears to be safe. If sellers of meat have more information about quality than consumers do, can consumers look after their interests? Yes; uneven information does not imply that sellers have an incentive to sell unsafe meat. Consumers are protected by the sellers' economic interests.

Private inspection firms, which must meet the market test, have a greater incentive to be effective than do government regulators.

The use of brand names, such as Armour or Swift, is one way that private firms assure quality standards for meat. A brand name enables consumers to identify a firm's meat product and choose it over competitors. Hence, a firm with an established and valuable brand name has a strong financial incentive to adhere to quality standards.

A company responsible for selling contaminated meat can be quickly ruined by adverse publicity about its products. The recall of Hudson beef in 1997 left Burger King branches across the midwest without hamburgers. Following the recall, Burger King canceled their contract with Hudson Foods and announced that it would never buy from the company again—showing that it is strongly in the financial interest of business firms not to sell tainted meat.

Where quality is difficult for consumers to evaluate, little-known firms may benefit from the services of private inspectors to certify safety. There is considerable evidence that market forces can assure product quality without government regulation. Best Western, for example, is a private certification agency that enables travelers to identify motels that meet specified quality standards. Underwriters Laboratories establishes standards for electrical products, and tests them to see if they meet those standards. These examples show that firms frequently are willing to pay to assure customers that their products meet prescribed standards. The success of *Consumer Reports* and similar publications is further evidence that consumers are willing to pay to be informed.

Is meat inspection an exception to the rule that private firms generally perform more effectively than government? There are good reasons to think that market-based inspection of the meat industry could improve on the current system. Illness associated with contaminated meat often occurs with federal meat inspection. There is no way, of course, to prevent all food-related illness. Mistakes on the part of buyers and sellers, and some degree of fraud, are unavoidable whatever the institutional arrangement. The goal in meat inspection, as in other areas of economic activity, is to establish an institutional arrangement that provides and uses information in a way that best serves consumers. The free market generally is more effective than government regulation in doing so.

Why not more market inspection of meat?

We've seen that businesses and consumers are willing to pay to assure product quality. And, as emphasized throughout, it is apparent that private inspection agencies "have a lot going for them." Yet, despite the ostensible advantages of the market approach, there is little reliance on market forces in meat inspection in the United States. Why does the meat industry not rely on market regulation more?

Market-generated information about the quality of meat undoubtedly would be much greater in the absence of government regulation. Government inspection tends to preempt market inspection, much as taxpayer-financed education crowds out privately funded schools, by reducing the incentives of sellers and buyers to look after safety on their own. There is little demand on the part of meat handlers for services that would be provided by private firms in the absence of government inspection. Business firms are, of course, also happy to have the taxpayers pick up the tab for inspection.

Similarly, with assurances by the USDA (and the media) that government regulation is crucial to consumer safety, there is little impetus for consumers to change the current institutional arrangement. Moreover, when problems of meat safety occur, there is no discussion of "government failure." Instead, regulatory officials plead for more power. In the aftermath of the Hudson Foods incident, for example, Secretary Glickman requested additional authority to shut down food-processing plants and to impose fines of $100,000 per day on any plant not obeying his order.

There can be no guarantees when it comes to food safety. Indeed, zero risk is not a reasonable objective in any aspect of human action. There are two approaches to ensuring the safety of meat—market inspection and government regulation. It is ironic that the public expects government regulation, which has more imperfections than the competitive market process, to provide for meat safety. Few people question the appropriateness of government regulation of the meat industry, even when they fault its effectiveness.

No one has a stronger interest in protecting consumers from tainted meat than the businesses in the industry. Ultimately, safety is best assured when rooted in the self-interest of business firms and consumers.

15

Too Much Responsibility for Food Safety Is Placed on Consumers

Sandra B. Eskin, Nancy Donley, Donna Rosebaum, and Karen Taylor Mitchell

Sandra B. Eskin is a writer and consultant on food safety issues. Nancy Donley is president of Safe Tables Our Priority (STOP). Donna Rosebaum is cofounder of STOP and a food safety advocate. Karen Taylor Mitchell is executive director of STOP. STOP is a nonprofit organization that assists victims of food-borne illnesses and advocates for food safety.

Government and food industry officials are sending consumers mixed messages; they insist that America has the safest food in the world and then try to convince consumers that they have to take special precautions in cooking and storing food so it will be safe to eat. Further, inaccurate or incomplete labeling may lead consumers to believe that food is safe and "ready to eat" when cooking may be necessary, particularly for vulnerable consumers—pregnant women, the very old or the very young, and people with compromised immune systems. Finally, too much emphasis is placed on consumer education and the responsibility of consumers to protect themselves from unsafe foods. The best way to reduce the incidence of food-borne illnesses is to keep pathogens from contaminating the food supply before it ever reaches consumers.

Food safety agencies, as well as food industry trade associations, have made extensive investments in consumer education since 1993. In 1998, the government established a website, www.foodsafety.gov, for food safety resources. Food safety messages such as "It's safe to bite when the temperature's right" are appropriate and useful, and academic studies have shown that consumer knowledge regarding certain foods, pathogens, and handling procedures has increased dramatically over the past decade. However, a number of problems exist with current consumer education efforts.

Mixed messages

Government and industry officials at all levels constantly send mixed messages to the public. With government officials and industry leaders incessantly repeating the unsubstantiated mantra, "we have the safest food supply in the world," foodborne illness victims in particular and consumers in general are unprepared to believe that they are at significant risk from pathogenic bacteria in the food they eat. Attempts to change people's behavior are doomed to fail when they are being told there is no problem.

Similarly, consumers are being given mixed messages about what constitutes safe food handling behavior. They read about a product recall but are also told that no illnesses have been associated with it, leading them to question whether a real problem exists. Furthermore, recall information is juxtaposed with information stating that it's safe to eat contaminated product as long as you cook it right. As a result, it is reasonable for consumers to conclude, "It must not be that bad or they'd tell us not to eat it at all." To make matters worse, numerous studies have shown that knowledge of food safety hazards is not translating into behavioral changes sufficient to protect most families from contaminated food.

Government-sponsored consumer education initiatives send mixed messages to the public, and place too much emphasis on the responsibility of consumers to protect themselves from foodborne illness.

Product labels also send mixed messages. Consumers reasonably presume that a product is safe when it is stamped "Inspected by the USDA" [United States Department of Agriculture] on a product label, when this may not be the case. Products that are labeled "ready to eat," are, in fact, not ready to eat, particularly for vulnerable consumers—older persons, pregnant women, and people with suppressed immune systems—who are especially susceptible to *Listeriosis*. Among other products, notably fresh produce, warning and handling labels are conspicuously absent, as is information about the food's origin that could help consumers assess its safety.

Moreover, key messages are either missing from or underemphasized in current consumer education initiatives. The most important of these is the extensive threat posed by cross-contamination. The fact that precious educational resources are targeted at young schoolchildren blatantly ignores the reality that they are not the ones who prepare the food.

Blaming the victim

Most significant here is the fact that the current food-safety strategy followed by both the government and industry places far too much emphasis on consumer intervention. The overemphasis on consumer education fosters the misleading impression that it is consumers' responsibility to make sure that their food is safe, and that, if people get sick, it's their own fault. The contradictory nature of USDA's dual missions—to both market meat and protect the public—is particularly relevant here, as shown by the 1998 USDA Annual Report, which recast the foodborne illness awareness and educational goals of the 1997 Presidential directive as "Raising Consumers' Confidence in Food Safety."

Consumer education should not be a substitute for measures that would prevent microbial contamination and its proliferation in food production and transportation.

An industry-government partnership called FightBac, instituted in 1997, perhaps best demonstrates the educational misfire. A major originator of consumer information, the FightBac campaign delivers the message to consumers to "keep your food safe from bacteria." Yet, this message is more appropriately delivered to the food industry itself. Consumers cannot keep their food safe from most deadly pathogenic contamination; at best they can merely mitigate the effects of prior contamination. To that extent, the government must provide consumers with complete and realistic information about food contamination and foodborne disease in the United States, consistently do all it can throughout the food production chain to "keep consumers safe from bacteria in food," and implement effective behavioral change models to help consumers effectively mitigate risks until preventable contamination is under control.

There is no question that consumers can compound or even create food safety problems through cross-contamination, undercooking, and improper thawing or cooling. However, government-sponsored consumer education initiatives send mixed messages to the public, and place too much emphasis on the responsibility of consumers to protect themselves from foodborne illness. The most direct and effective solution to the problem is to keep the pathogens out of the food supply in the first place. Consumer education should not be a substitute for measures that would prevent microbial contamination and its proliferation in food production and transportation.

Workable recommendations

• Educational messages relating to food safety must be consistent, truthful, and complete, and they must explain the problem as well as promote techniques to minimize risk from foodborne pathogens.

• Research is needed to enhance the effectiveness of food safety education on consumer behavior modification before further resources are expended on efforts which fail to reduce the toll of foodborne disease.

• Special attention should be paid to developing educational initiatives directed at subpopulations with particularly high incidences of severe foodborne illness.

Organizations to Contact

The editors have compiled the following list of organizations concerned with the issues debated in this book. The descriptions are derived from materials provided by the organizations. All have publications or information available for interested readers. The list was compiled on the date of publication of the present volume; the information provided here may change. Be aware that many organizations take several weeks or longer to respond to inquiries, so allow as much time as possible.

American Council on Science and Health (ACSH)
1995 Broadway, 2nd Fl., New York, NY 10023-5860
(212) 362-7044 • fax: (212) 362-4919
e-mail: acsh@acsh.org • website: www.acsh.org

ACSH provides consumers with scientific evaluations of food and the environment, pointing out both health hazards and benefits. It participates in a variety of government and media events, from congressional hearings to popular magazines. It publishes the bimonthly *News and Views*, as well as the booklets *Eating Safely: Avoiding Foodborne Illness*, *Biotechnology and Food*, and *Modernize the Food Safety Laws: Delete the Delaney Clause*.

Biotechnology Industry Organization (BIO)
1625 K St. NW, Suite 1100, Washington, DC 20006
(202) 857-0244 • fax: (202) 857-0237
e-mail: info@bio.org • website: www.bio.org

BIO represents biotechnology companies, academic institutions, and state biotechnology centers engaged in the development of products and services in the areas of biomedicine, agriculture, and environmental applications. It conducts workshops and produces educational activities aimed at increasing public understanding of biotechnology. Its publications include the bimonthly newsletter *BIO Bulletin*, the periodical *BIO News*, and the book *Biotech for All*.

Campaign for Food Safety (CFS)
860 Hwy. 61, Little Marais, MN 55614
(218) 226-4164 • fax: (218) 226-4157
e-mail: alliance@mr.net • website: www.purefood.org

The Campaign for Food Safety promotes the growth of organic and sustainable agriculture practices. CFS activist strategies include education, boycotts, grassroots lobbying, litigation, networking, direct-action protests, and media events. It publishes the newsletter *Campaign for Food Safety News* as well as the periodic *Action Alerts*.

Center for Science in the Public Interest (CSPI)
1875 Connecticut Ave. NW, Suite 300, Washington, DC 20009
(202) 332-9110 • fax: (202) 265-4954
e-mail: cspi@cspinet.org • website: www.cspinet.org

The Center for Science in the Public Interest is a nonprofit education and advocacy organization committed to improving the safety and nutritional quality of the U.S. food supply. It publishes *Nutrition Action Healthletter,* the largest-circulation health newsletter in the country.

Food and Drug Administration (FDA)
5600 Fishers Lane, Rockville, MD 20857
(888) 463-6332
e-mail: webmail@oc.fda.gov • website: www.fda.gov

The FDA is a public health agency, charged with protecting American consumers by enforcing the Federal Food, Drug, and Cosmetic Act and several related public health laws. To carry out this mandate of consumer protection, the FDA has investigators and inspectors covering the country's almost ninety-five thousand FDA-regulated businesses. Its publications include government documents, reports, fact sheets, and press announcements.

Food Safety Consortium (FSC)
110 Agriculture Building, University of Arkansas, Fayetteville, AR 72701
(501) 575-5647 • fax: (501) 575-7531
e-mail: fsc@cavern.uark.edu • website: www.uark.edu/depts/fsc

Congress established the Food Safety Consortium, consisting of researchers from the University of Arkansas, Iowa State University, and Kansas State University, in 1988 through a special Cooperative State Research Service grant. It conducts extensive investigation into all areas of poultry, beef, and pork meat production. The consortium publishes the quarterly *FSC Newsletter.*

Friends of the Earth (FoE)
1025 Vermont Ave. NW, No. 300, Washington, DC 20005
(202) 783-7400 • fax: (202) 783-0444
e-mail: foe@foe.org • website: www.foe.org

Friends of the Earth monitors legislation and regulations that affect the environment. Its Safer Food, Safer Farms Campaign speaks out against what it perceives as the negative impact biotechnology can have on farming, food production, genetic resources, and the environment. It publishes the quarterly newsletter *Atmosphere* and the magazine *Friends of the Earth* ten times a year.

International Vegetarian Union (IVU)
PO Box 9710, Washington, DC 20016
(202) 362-8349
e-mail: vuna@ivu.org • website: www.ivu.org

The International Vegetarian Union is a nonprofit organization which advocates animal welfare, humanitarian, and health objectives. It publishes the annual *IVU News* and makes available on its website articles concerning food safety issues from affiliate vegetarian organizations.

National Cattlemen's Beef Association (NCBA)
5420 S. Quebec St., Greenwood Village, CO 80111-1905
(303) 694-0305 • fax: (303) 694-2851
e-mail: cattle@beef.org • website: www.beef.org

National Cattlemen's Beef Association is the marketing organization and trade association for America's 1 million cattle farmers and ranchers. Its Food Safety library publishes the quarterly *Food and Nutrition* newsletter, the fact sheet "Progress in Food Safety: Toward a Safer Beef Supply," and the booklet *Plating It Safe.*

National Food Safety Database
University of Florida
3082 McCarty Hall B, PO Box 110287, Gainesville, FL 32611
(352) 846-2270 • fax: (352) 846-1102
e-mail: alla@gnv.ifas.ufl.edu • website: www.foodsafety.org

The National Food Safety Database project is an organization funded primarily by the USDA in order to develop an efficient management system of U.S. food safety databases. Numerous food safety fact sheets, including "Preventing Foodborne Illnesses," "Myths About Food Safety," and "Botulism—It Only Takes a Taste," are available on its website.

Organic Consumers Association (OCA)
6101 Cliff Estate Rd., Little Marais, MN 55614
(218) 226-4164 • fax: (218) 353-7652
website: www.organicconsumers.org

The OCA is a grassroots nonprofit public interest organization that deals with crucial issues of food safety, industrial agriculture, genetic engineering, corporate accountability, and environmental sustainability. The OCA is the only organization in the United States focused exclusively on representing the views and interests of the nation's estimated 10 million organic consumers. The association publishes three newsletters, *Biodemocarcy, Organic Views,* and *Organic Bytes,* as well as fact sheets including "Hazards of G.E. Foods and Crops."

Safe Tables Our Priority (STOP)
PO Box 4352, Burlington, VT 05406
(802) 863-0555 • fax: (802) 863-3733
e-mail: mail@safetables.org • website: www.stop-usa.org

Safe Tables Our Priority is a nonprofit organization devoted to victim assistance, public education, and policy advocacy for safe food and public health. STOP's mission is to prevent unnecessary illness and loss of life from pathogenic food-borne illness. STOP's publications include newsletters, policy statements, testimonies, and press releases. The organization also offers several pamphlets including *What Is Foodborne Disease* and *The Problem Is Unsafe Food,* as well as a report, *Why Are People Still Dying from Contaminated Food?*

U.S. Department of Agriculture (USDA) Food Safety and Inspection Service (FSIS)
1400 Independence Ave. SW, Room 2932-S, Washington, DC 20250-3700
(202) 720-7943 • fax: (202) 720-1843
e-mail: fsiswebmaster@usda.gov • website: www.fsis.usda.gov

The Food Safety and Inspection Service is the public health agency of the USDA responsible for ensuring that the nation's commercial supply of meat, poultry, and egg products is safe, wholesome, and correctly labeled and packaged. It publishes fact sheets, reports, articles, and brochures on food safety topics.

Bibliography

Books

Peter Cerexhe and John Ashton — *Risky Food, Safer Choices*. New South Wales, Australia: New South Wales University, 1999.

Madeline Drexler — *Secret Agent*. Washington, DC: National Academy Press, 2002.

Lawrence J. Dyckman and Erin J. Lansburgh — *Meat and Poultry*. Collingdale, PA: DIANE, 2002.

Thomas W. Frazier and Drew C. Richardson, eds. — *Food and Agricultural Security: Guarding Against Natural Threats and Terrorist Attacks Affecting Health, National Foods Supplies, and Agricultural Economies*. New York: New York Academy of Sciences, 2000.

Robert H. Gates — *Infectious Disease Secrets*. Philadelphia, PA: Elsevier, 2003.

Kathleen Hart — *Eating in the Dark: America's Experiment with Genetically Engineered Food*. New York: Alfred A. Knopf, 2003.

Knut J. Heller — *Genetically Engineered Food: Detection of Genetic Modification*. New York: John Wiley and Sons, 2003.

Rebecca Hohlstein — *Food Fight: The Battle to Protect Our Food and Water Against Terrorism*. Madison, WI: Goblin Fern Press, 2003.

Mick Isle — *Everything You Need to Know About Food Poisoning*. New York: Rosen, 2000.

Bill Lambrecht — *Dinner at the New Gene Café: How Genetic Engineering Is Changing What We Eat, How We Live, and the Global Politics of Food*. New York: St. Martin's Press, 2001.

Warren Leon — *Is Our Food Safe?* New York: Crown/Three Rivers Press, 2002.

Marion Nestle — *Safe Food: Bacteria, Biotechnology, and Bioterrorism*. Berkeley: University of California Press, 2003.

Michael T. Osterholm and John Schwartz — *Living Terrors: What America Needs to Know to Survive the Coming Bioterrorist Catastrophe*. New York: Dell, 2001.

Thomas Peacock — *Is It Safe to Eat Out? How Our Local Health Officials Inspect Restaurants to Assure Food Safety . . . or Do They?* Lincoln, NE: Writer's Showcase Press, 2002.

Peter Pringle — *Food, Inc.: Mendel to Monsanto—the Promises and Perils of the Biotech Harvest*. New York: Simon & Schuster, 2003.

Maxine Rosaler — *Botulism*. New York: Rosen, 2003.

74

Andrew Rowell   *Don't Worry, It's Safe to Eat; the True Story of GM Food, BSE, and Foot-and-Mouth Disease.* London: Earthscan, 2003.

Eric Schlosser   *Fast Food Nation: The Dark Side of the All-American Meal.* Boston: Houghton Mifflin, 2001.

Maxine Schwartz   *How the Cows Turned Mad.* Berkeley: University of California Press, 2003.

Charlotte A. Spencer   *Mad Cows and Cannibals: A Guide to the Transmissible Spongiform Encephalopatries.* Upper Saddle River, NJ: Prentice-Hall, 2003.

John Stauber   *Mad Cow USA.* Monroe, ME: Common Courage Press, 2003.

Jill Trickett   *The Prevention of Food Poisoning.* Cheltenham, England: Stanley Thornes, 2001.

U.S. Government   *The Future of Food.* Washington, DC: U.S. Government
Printing Office   Printing Office, 2000.

Periodicals

Joel Bleifuss   "A 21st Century Plague? Britain's Mad Cows May Harbinger the Deaths of Millions," *In These Times*, February 7, 2000.

Edith A. Chenault   "Scientists Charged with Helping to Prevent Food-Borne Illness," *Texas A&M Agricultural News*, February 10, 2000. www.agnews.tamu.edu.

Mary H. Cooper   "Mad Cow Disease," *CQ Researcher*, March 2, 2001. Available from 1414 22nd St. NW, Washington, DC 20037.

Council on   "Food and Agriculture," *Terrorism Q & A*, 2003.
Foreign Relations

Environmental Health "The New System for Seafood Safety," October 1998.
Perspectives

Thom Hartmann   "No Place to Escape," *Tikkun*, May/June 1999.

David Hosansky   "Food Safety," *CQ Researcher*, November 1, 2002.

Issues and Controversies "Update: Food Safety," February 20, 1998. Available
On File   from Facts On File News Service, 11 Penn Plaza, New York, NY 10001-2006.

Journal of   "Dramatic Decline in Foodborne Illness," December
Environmental Health 2002.

Heather Klinkhamer   "Globalization I: How Should the FDA Ensure the Safety of Imported Foods," testimony at the 21st Annual National Food Policy Conference, March 24, 1998. www.stop-usa.org.

Joseph P. Lewandowski "Food Terrorism Potential Small but Worrisome," *Natural Foods Merchandiser*, January 2002. www.newhope.com.

Kathryn McConnell   "U.S. Regulatory Process Ensures Food Safety, Officials Say," U.S. Embassy, Japan, November 14, 2002. www.tokyo.usembassy.gov.

New Zealand   "Food Borne Illnessess," September 2000.
Ministry of Health   www.moh.govt.nz.

Milford Prewitt   "USDA to Confab: Food Supply Safe from Terror; Veneman Says Pipeline Well Protected," *Nation's Restaurant News*, March 31, 2003.

Bryan Salvage   "Activist Law Firm Lobbying for Hepatitis A Vaccination Program," *Outbreak*, March 15, 2001. www.outbreakinc.com.

Susan Bourque Seward   "Food Service Hand Washing Versus Glove Use: A Food Safety Perspective," *Dietetic Intern*, December 2000. www.dieteticintern.com.

James H. Steele   "Food Irradiation: A Public Health Measure Long Overdue!" *21st* Century, Fall 1999.

Miriam E. Tucker   "AMA Primer to Promote Management, Prevention of Food-Borne Illnesses," *Family Practice News*, February 15, 2001.

University of Georgia   "Food-Borne Illnesses Under Attack," *Return on*
College of Agriculture   *Investment*, 2001. www.agcomm.uga.edu.
and Environmental
Sciences

U.S. Department   "The Animal and Plant Health Inspection Service and
of Agriculture   the Department of Homeland Security: Working Together to Protect Agriculture," *APHIS Factsheet*, May 2003.

U.S. Department   "Consumer Food Safety Behavior: Consumer Demand
of Agriculture   for Food Safety," *Briefing Room*, June 5, 2002. www.ers.usda.gov/Briefing.

U.S. Food and   "FDA Issues Final Two Proposed Food Safety
Drug Administration   Regulations," May 6, 2003. www.cfsan.fda.gov.

Donovan Webster   "The Stink About Pork," *George*, April 1999. Available from 30 Montgomery St., Jersey City, NJ 07032.

World Health   "Terrorists Threats to Food: Guidance for Establishing
Organization   and Strengthening Prevention and Response Systems," 2002. www.who.int/fsf.

Catherine E. Woteki   "Safeguarding America's Meat," *Ripon Forum*, Summer 2001.

Index